Squeekie Celebrates 20 Years of Cupboard Maker Books

SQUEEKIE THE BOOKSTORE CAT

with help from his friends

Copyright © 2018 Squeekie the Bookstore Cat

Second Edition Copyright © 2019

All rights reserved

ISBN: 978-0-578-41444-7

DEDICATION

To everyone who stops to pet me and give me treats,
and to everyone who read my first two books.
This book wouldn't be possible without you.

CONTENTS

	Acknowledgements	i
1.	Squeekie's New Ghost	1
	Misty Simon	
2.	Squeekie Goes to the Farm	9
	Michelle Haring	
3.	Squeekie and Bingo	17
	Samantha Coons	
4.	The Perfect Match	31
	Carrie Jacobs	
5.	Squeekie Goes to the Horse Barn	37
	Kristian Beverly	
6.	Squeekie and the Lost Human	45
	Katie Twigg	
7.	My Distant Love	53
	Heidi Hormel	
8.	A Purrfect Tribute	65
	Andrew Coons	
Note about stories 9-20		**77**
9.	Way of the Beloved Kitty	79
	Heidi Hormel	

10.	Hide and Go Squeek	89
	Eric Hardenbrook	
11.	Squeekie vs. the Stinkie Apocalypse	95
	Jay Smith	
12.	The Drunken Comic Book Monkeys vs. Squeekie	111
	Brian Koscienski & Chris Pisano	
13.	Everybody Needs a Friend	119
	Carrie Jacobs	
14.	Squeekie Saves the Store	127
	Natalie J. Damschroder	
15.	Squeekie and the Kitten	133
	Samantha Coons	
16.	A Friend like Squeekie	141
	Melissa Ford	
17.	Squeekie and the Little Horses	147
	Kristian Beverly	
18.	Squeekie and the Mermaid	153
	Lynne Reeder	
19.	Squeekie and the Ghosts	161
	Michelle Haring	
20.	Squeekie and His Friends	169
	Katie Twigg	

ACKNOWLEDGEMENTS

A big thank you to all the Humans who wrote this book for me.

1

Squeekie's New Ghost

Misty Simon

As the Bookstore Cat, it was my job to know who came and went in my home. And I took my job very seriously.

Cupboard Maker Books had many people who came in, excited to buy new books and share the ones they'd loved. They talked plots and imaginary people all day long with my humans who worked at the store and especially my main human, Michelle. I was fine with this as long as they also petted me and told me I was pretty. Since I was definitely pretty, this was not an issue.

Even though I liked most of the people, I wasn't too sure about this woman who kept lifting me up from the counter and measuring the length of my legs.

"I bet I could find something really cute for your Squeekie. He'd be the hit of any party with costumes galore. I'm expanding my business down in Virginia, but I could ship to you."

Michelle laughed as I squinted at her. "Thanks, Ivy, but I don't know if Squeekie would be good in a costume."

So she meant to put me in one of those funny clothes things that made you look like something else? I shook my head, which jingled the bell around my neck. Bowties and collars were enough for me, thank you very much.

But for once Michelle did not get my message. "Though maybe he would like that. He seems excited at the thought."

I jumped up on the printer next to the cash register and told her how very much I did not approve of that idea. She ignored me as the lady who was going to give our store a good spring cleaning came in and stood at the counter with Ivy and Michelle.

Misty Simon

Once Michelle introduced the out-of-towner (thank goodness because she wouldn't be around to measure me anymore) to the cleaning lady who knew how to scratch behind my ears just right, the two new humans smiled at each other and started talking books. Of course they did.

"I love a good mystery, Tallie," the one named Ivy said.

The other one squeezed her arm. "Me, too. Are you new around here? I know just about everyone, but I've ever seen you before."

Ivy shook her head. See, it was supposed to mean "no", not "yes, please, put me in a stupid dragon costume for Halloween".

"No, my family and I are just up here for the weekend to visit my husband's cousin. I can't resist a book store, especially one that has beautiful books painted on the side of the building. I made Ben turn a sharp right as soon as I saw them."

Tallie laughed, and I moved away. Why stay when no one was paying attention to me? And maybe if the Ivy lady couldn't see me, she'd forget all about sending me costumes. I was perfect just the way I was, or so everyone told me.

As I rounded the corner, a guy came in the store with a big box of books under his arm. The two ladies moved away so Michelle could check out what he wanted to trade in for store credit.

His face was sad and his shoulders rounded. I wondered what his story was.

"My mother passed last week, and she said in her will that all her books were supposed to come to you. I've got a whole truck load out there." He jerked his thumb over his shoulder. "Where do you want them?"

"I'm so sorry your mother passed away." Michelle's smile was gentle as she opened the first box and started sorting through the treasures. It grew in that way it did when she knew she had some awesome books coming in the store that her friends would love.

"Will they go to good homes?" the man asked with his own sad smile.

"Absolutely. Thank you."

"She'd love that."

"Bring the rest in. We'll get them sorted out."

Squeekie's New Ghost

I sauntered off to climb through the overhead wooden trails at that point since business was being done, and I wasn't needed.

I spent the rest of the day just hanging out and getting to know the new temporary cat that had been dropped off yesterday. They were all the same color but not related. I hoped I would be able to tell them apart for as long as they were here. Normally, that wasn't long. Michelle was very good at not only finding good homes for books but also for cats who needed to find their forever home, like I had.

And then night came, and the lights were turned off, and the people all said goodbye. It was the same every night, so I no longer minded it. It had bothered me in the beginning, but with the darkness came my other friends. These ones I could see through, but they weren't imaginary.

I used to talk to the other bookstore cat, Annika, but she was standoffish now and ran away whenever I tried to be near her. It left me alone a lot during the night hours.

Fortunately, there were other permanent residents of the book store. Three ghosts lived with us. At first I wasn't sure what to do with them. There was Bob who had worked on the railroad. He was the nicest and talked to me the most. There was a sad-eyed girl who didn't say much, just looked ragged and so lost. And then there was the creepy ghost who lived in the basement. I tried not to interact with him if I didn't have to.

But when the lights went off this time, there was a new ghost in the store. How did she get in here? She was faded like the rest, but smiling too. She walked from the back as if she owned the place and actually said hi right to me without me having to chase her down and ask for her story.

She told me her name was Lovey and it sounded so pretty as she tickled my belly that I purred. For three nights she worked to fit in with the other ghosts. The smile on her face never wavered as she traded stories with Bob and managed to get the sad girl to talk a few times. I wasn't there to hear the story but then maybe I wasn't meant to be.

Then Monday, after I had dinner, a lady with strange hair and lace gloves that caught in my fur when she rubbed my back walked in.

She was quick to apologize but then immediately went to find Michelle. I followed along behind her because nothing else exciting was going on. Right now, we only had one new kitten in the store. I'd been working on teaching him to stay inside but other than that, he didn't ever want to do anything but see how far his claws could stretch out. Boring!

The lady and I went into the back room after she ooh'd and aah'd over the yellow brick road painted on the floor. She kept muttering to herself that she'd have to come back some day when she wasn't on a mission. What mission? What was she here for?

Curiosity definitely got this cat. I wound my way around her ankles as we went to find Michelle. She was in the back behind the curtain with all those books that people loved to read with happy endings. I'd found mine here at the store so I thought other people deserved theirs too.

"Are you Michelle?" the lady with the poofy hair asked.

I could have told her that if only she'd asked me.

"I am," Michelle answered. "Can I help you?"

"Um, I'm not sure how to go about this."

Michelle raised her eyebrows and crossed her arms. That was the stance she sometimes took when I did bad things so I waited to see what would happen next.

"I'd say straightforward would be best." Michelle glanced down at me then looked back at the lady.

"Right, bad foot, bad start. Sorry. I'm new to chasing down things and I have got to get better at this."

"Chasing down things? What are you chasing down?"

The lady straightened her lace gloves and cleared her throat. "A book, actually. One book in particular. I'm told it was dropped off here a few days ago by a man who had things from his mother's estate."

Michelle looked curious now too. "One book in particular? Why that one? There were some first editions in the boxes, but I haven't had a chance to go through everything yet."

Squeekie's New Ghost

"I can tell you which book as soon as I see them."

"Wait, so you have to see them? Don't you even know the name of the book?"

Just then Lovey showed up behind Michelle. She was still smiling, but now it looked a little sad. "You're looking for me, aren't you?" she said right to the woman. Right to her!

"Yes," the lady said, looking at Lovey instead of Michelle.

I'd never seen any other human talk to my ghostly friends. Could she see her? Talk to her? How did this work? I hadn't seen her eat any catnip like I had to in order to talk to the ghosts, so how was she doing it?

Michelle continued to look at the lady with the big hair because she couldn't hear the ghost talking at her shoulder.

"Uh, yes. I'm sorry I don't know the name of the book, just the binding," the lady said, looking at Michelle again.

Michelle stepped back a little because this lady was now talking super loud even for my ears.

"Fleishmann's Hike," Lovey said then sat down on the floor. "I suppose you have to take me with you now, don't you? I've just made friends, and I like it here, and they have this lovely feline. I've been boxed up for so many years, I can't remember the last time I had this much fun, and now it's going to end."

I was so sad for Lovey that I howled and raced around Michelle's feet. I didn't know what I thought that would do, but sometimes you just have to follow your urges.

The lady looked down at me and winked at me. I caught it by accident, and it stopped me in my tracks.

"You know what? I don't think I need that book after all. If you ever come across anything that is weird or different though, give me a call. I'm happy to help with moving any book that just doesn't feel like it belongs in your store."

"You're not going to make me go?" Lovey rose from the floor in one smooth motion.

The lady shook her head. "Nice to meet you, Michelle. You have a great store and great occupants."

"Um, thanks." Michelle squinted at the card in her hand. "Mel, is it? You're an antique dealer?"

"That's what the cards say." She shrugged and smiled. "If you ever need any help, just let me know."

"Okay." But Michelle still sounded skeptical, which I guessed was okay. Mel trotted out of the store in her jelly shoes after throwing another wink in Lovey's direction.

Michelle followed her out to the front, probably to make sure she wasn't some loony bird. But she wasn't, she just was able to see things differently. And without catnip! Go figure.

"Who was that Mel person?" I asked Lovey, curling up at her feet. She stroked her hand down my back, not that I could feel it but I watched it because it made me feel good.

"She's a ghost hunter. She comes and takes objects that people are attached to and helps ghosts go on to the next phase."

"Oh, and you didn't want to leave?"

"Not after meeting you and getting to know Resa. Bob is okay, too, but that thing downstairs has to go. Maybe we should leave Michelle a note to call Mel back and give her whatever he's attached to!"

"That might be a great idea."

"It is a great idea, my Squeekie. And then Resa would probably talk again and not look so sad. See, problems solved. Now, why don't you show me what you can do on that catwalk again? You're so pretty when you're up there."

"First I have to find your book and hide it away so no one can take you out of the store," I said.

"I can show you right where it is."

"Good. And then I'll show you all the fun catwalks."

"I'd love that."

After finding the book and hiding it where no one would ever find it, I preened, and I purred. And in the end I performed for my new friend, Lovey, who was going to be a permanent friend now. You could never have too many of those.

Squeekie's New Ghost

AUTHOR BIOGRAPHY

Misty Simon always wanted to be a storyteller...preferably behind a Muppet. Animal was number one, followed closely by Sherlock Hemlock... Since that dream didn't come true, she began writing stories to share her world with readers, one laugh at a time. She knows how to hula, was classically trained to sing opera, co-wrote her high school *Alma Mater,* and can't touch raw wood. Never hand her a Dixie cup with that wooden spoon/paddle thing. It's not pretty.

Touching people's hearts and funny bones are two of her favorite things, and she hopes everyone at least snickers in the right places when reading her books. She lives with her husband, daughter, and two insane dogs in Central Pennsylvania where she is hard at work on her next novel or three. She loves to hear from readers so drop her a line at misty@mistysimon.com.

Squeekie the Bookstore Cat

2

Squeekie Goes to the Farm

Michelle Haring

Squeekie, the book store cat here. I want to introduce myself. I love people and books and other cats. I also love adventures. My person, Michelle, is happy about my love of people, books and cats but she doesn't approve of my adventures. She thinks that I should always stay inside the bookstore and never go to explore other places.

Last year, when she was not here, I used to sneak outside when my farmer friends visited during the time when the sun was new. My farmer friends brought so many boxes with green lids and purple lids for me to smell and rub against. They would also prop open the door to the outside. I used to follow them and eat the pretty, bright green grass that I watched through my glass door.

Then one day I heard one of them say, "We love your outdoor cat. He's so friendly."

Michelle replied, "What outdoor cat? I don't have any outdoor cat."

The nice farmer said, "The Siamese looking guy with the sleek body, gorgeous tan coat and striking blue eyes."

At least that is how he described me in my interpretation.

He may have actually said, "The sort of tan cat."

Michelle nodded and glared at me with a funny look on her face.

The next week on the night before the farmers came, Michelle hurt my dignity, my pride and my feelings. She put me in kitty jail. Kitty jail is the place where the new cats sleep. They go there so they can adjust to the sounds, smells and people of the bookstore. This my home, I know exactly what everything smells like. It smells like me. I'm the one who rubs on everything and claims it all. I claim the bookcases, the books and the people, especially the people.

Oh the indignity of being locked up in kitty jail for an entire night. She looked at me that first night and said, "Everyone loves you too much to bear the thought of losing you. The bookstore is right along the highway and across from the train tracks. If you wander off, we would all be sad. So, you go to kitty jail to keep you from bothering the farmers."

The next morning, the farmers came and I cried because I wanted to play with my friends. They came to the edge of kitty jail and one said, "Wow buddy, I'm not sure what you did but we're sorry that you're locked in here."

I cried and cried but they didn't understand my long explanation of Michelle's worries. They discussed letting me free but they didn't. When Michelle got to the store, she opened the cage and let me out with a small sorry.

For most of the year, this became my pattern. Every Tuesday night, I got locked in jail. Sometimes it was even worse because I was locked with one of the temporary cats. The temporary cats live at my bookstore until they find their forever homes. The temporary cats have their own stories so I don't need to talk about them.

This is my store, my story and my adventure.

The farmers always come back the day after they drop the boxes to pick up the empty boxes. I don't get locked in my cage on the empty day because Michelle watches me and doesn't let me go outside. If I hang out at the door and she catches me, she sprays me with water. I don't like being sprayed. I used to hate it, but now I simply saunter away from door. It's like a game.

I love to sit on the boxes and rub on them. The boxes have the most interesting smells attached to them. Sometimes they smell like other cat but a different type of other cat. A cat that smells somehow freer than I am. Usually, the boxes smell like wonderful, amazing people food. The smells change throughout the year. When the deliveries start in April, the boxes from the farm smell like onions, radishes, greens, and potatoes. By June, they smell like cucumbers, parsley, tomatoes, and strawberries. By the end of summer in August, they smell like sweet corn, cantaloupes, and sweet, orange peppers.

The people that get the boxes pet me when Michelle doesn't chase me away from the front of the store. They talk about the harvest and how wonderful it is to get fresh, local, organic vegetables once a month. Sometimes people ask about the boxes.

The people say the farm is called Spiral Path Farm. They say it's about an hour away but I don't think I'd enjoy sitting in a car for that long.

Listening to Michelle speak about buying local and picking it up in different places in the area reminds me of cat food. I get hungry, Michelle or another human goes and picks up the food at a nearby pet food place. The new food comes back smelling like all sorts of creatures. Some food is put in a large bowl for more cats and a smaller bowl for myself and Annika. That's how I imagine it.

Michelle loves to tell people about how pretty the farm is. If she didn't also pet me in those moments I'd feel like she liked the farm more than me. She also notes that the farm has a few open days where people can come visit the farm and learn about growing food. She says it's important for people to know where their food comes from.

Sometimes I wish I knew where my food came from. I know where the bugs come from and sometimes I get to snack on them. They appear from under the bookcases. People say books are magic, but I think the cases are too. The farm always sounded so interesting that I hoped someday I would get to go there.

The chance of a lifetime rammed into me and I took it.

It all started with a spider.

A spider tugged its string coming out of its backend and landed on the cool floor. I lower myself to the ground, front end down, back end up and tail straight like it's reaching for the sky.

The rays of the sun cast slivers of light through the glass front of the store's door.

I fly through the air before landing and catching my snack. After eating my tasty spider treat I hop on top of a box and listen to the sound of the Spiral Path truck. It beeps as it backs up to the door.

    I didn't move when I heard the front open. Sometimes I pretend that I can't hear people when they tell me to move. I can hear them perfectly well, but sometimes I just don't feel like listening. I identify different types of trains and I know what some cars sound like Michelle's human, Jason, has a car covered in Twinkies with clothes on it. Then there's a car with me on it. And it's my car. But I can't drive it. People talk about the Squeekie car around me and sometimes ask me if I drive it. Since I don't speak human, I can't tell them how silly their question is. My legs can't reach the pedals. However, my Squeekie car is electric so it doesn't make any noise when it pulls up to the building. So sometimes Michelle surprises me when she comes into our store.

    Back to that fateful day, my farmer friends were here early to retrieve the boxes. Whoever got their vegetables didn't put the lid on the box tightly so I could sneak into it. Would the farmer notice me in the box with the lid covering only half? I stand in front of the box, knowing I don't have long to make a decision. The best cat to ask for advice lives with me. Annika. She would never acknowledge it but she's my best friend.

    She yawns, showing me her tiny sharp teeth, "Why would I help you? What's in it for me?"

    "Well, you'll get the store to yourself for a few hours."

    She sighs. It puffs up her fur even more. "That's not enough of an incentive. That just means that they'll bother me if they can't find you."

    I step closer to the box, mindful of the men standing outside of the door at the truck.

    I say, "I bet it'll be entertaining to watch the humans try to figure out where I am."

    Annika swats her tail and glares at me. This is her happy face. "Okay, I like it when the humans panic."

    I jump into the box and flatten myself in it. Annika whispers something but I can't hear it. The door opens, and the sounds outside amplify. I freeze, hoping that they don't find me. They can't find me. I'm so close to going on my well planned and well thought out adventure.

The sounds disappear as boxes are placed on top of mine. A few seconds later someone is carrying me, their breath coming out smooth.

The alarm to the door sounds. It's only a short beep and I know I've made it.

My legs sprawl out from under me when my box lands on something solid. A loud grating whine sounds before it hits something solid and the air feels tight.

It's warm in the back here, and the engine hums. The truck lurches forward.

I'm too scared to move. But eventually sitting in the truck gets to be boring. I press my body against the side until the box falls over and I spill out.

The first thing I notice is the mountain of boxes. Because they're swaying from side to side and could fall on me.

They do fall.

I freeze after the last box rights itself. What if they heard the disaster and found me? I wouldn't get to see everything then!

I'm happy I decided to take my adventure in September not July. It would have been sweltering in July.

The truck was full of boxes so we didn't stop at any other pickups. It feels like eternity. The truck's turning and swaying ways. We drive for hours and hours. It may have been just an hour because Michelle always told people the farm was an hour away from the bookstore. At the end the road becomes twisty and bumpy. I didn't like that part and worry starts to comb through my gut. If no one opens the truck when we got to the farm, it might get too hot.

Finally we stop and I hide behind one of the boxes. When a different farmer jumps into the box truck to get some boxes, I slink out of the truck and jump to the dirt packed lane. No one raises the alarm so my adventure continues.

I walk past a gigantic greenhouse with glass walls. I sneak in through the open door and plants sat on tables everywhere. I don't stay because a mist came down from the ceiling and I don't enjoy getting wet. I wander to another building where people pack food into boxes. It was so clean and bright. Someone notices me because she says, "Where did that cat come from? There aren't supposed to be farm cats in the packing house. He also doesn't look like any of the farm cats."

I run out because I don't like to stay where I'm not wanted. Plus I don't want anyone to notice me. I walk toward the fields. I stand on a hill and look at the different types of fields. They were so amazing, filled with more green than I ever saw in my life. The plants were all different heights. Before I can get to any of the fields, I there's an outdoor cat in front of me. His large frame and tabby coloring remind me of my old friend, Mac, who spent two years at the bookstore before finding his forever home. He meows, "What are you doing on *my* farm?"

I puff out my chest, "I'm Squeekie the bookstore cat and I'm on walkabout."

"Why did you pick my home as your place for walkabout?"

"The farmers pet me and tell me I'm pretty. Michelle always tells everyone how cool Spiral Path is. I thought it would be neat to visit. Plus I was able to hide in a box to get here."

He nods, "I understand. We do wonderful things here. I listen to my people, too. They talk about how most food is processes. Spiral Path Farm vegetables remind people of the connections of food to the earth."

The farm cat and I walk up to the farmhouse and sit on the porch. He tells me about his birth on the farm and his role. He makes sure that the mice, groundhogs, and anything else that'd eat or dig up vegetables stay away from the packing house, the greenhouse and the farmhouse. He thinks of himself as the House Protector. He puffs out his chest and says he's a working cat. I tell him that I work too but my work is more like marketing. I encourage people to like my store and come back to it. I like all of the people even the small, loud ones. They pat me and sometimes drool on me but attention is attention.

I guess we take up too space because we draw the attention of the farmers. A man I don't recognize leans down to pet and asks who I am and where I came from. As a human, he can't understand my reply. I twine between his legs and explain my adventure but he doesn't understand cat. The farm cat watches with amusement dancing in his eyes.

A woman comes out of the house and says, "We just got a call. Michelle from the bookstore is missing her cat. His name is Squeekie. Have you seen him?"

As she asks the question, she looks down and sees me. She crouches to pet me, "You must be Squeekie. You're so nice and pretty. No wonder your person sounded panicked on the telephone. I'll call her right back. It sounded like she was crying."

I enjoyed my adventure but I don't want Michelle to be sad, so I sit down on the porch. The lady came out a minute later. She told me Michelle would be here as soon as possible. Based on my trip, I knew that it would take Michelle at least an hour or two to get to me, but I didn't want to inconvenience anyone any more so I curl up on the porch and take a nap.

When I hear the Minion car pull up to the farmhouse, I wake up. Michelle jumps out of the car and runs up to pull me into her arms.

She croons, "Squeekie, I love you but you were such a bad kitty."

She carries me back to the car and plops me into a carrier. She goes back to the porch and I hear her apologize for my behavior and having to leave so fast. She says, "Thank you all so much. I left my mom in the store and she doesn't want to be there."

The nice owners of Spiral Path assure her that it was okay.

On the ride home Michelle tells me that I frightened her but she still loves me. I try to tell her about my adventures but she still doesn't understand cat. After we leave the farm lane, Michelle turns on an audio book in which the woman's words ring like poetry. Michelle says, "Squeekie, I don't want to hear anything else from you. We're listening to her story so I can calm down and put this situation in proper perspective."

When we get back to the store, she puts me in kitty jail. She says I can think about my behavior. I try to tell Annika about my grand adventure, but she just yawns. No one understands my grand adventure except for me. Instead, I stay in kitty jail for a whole week while Michelle tells everyone about it wrong. She just focuses on the effect it had on her. She clearly missed that it was all about me.

Michelle Haring

AUTHOR BIOGRAPHY

Michelle Haring is the co-owner of Cupboard Maker Books. She loves all cats but especially Squeekie. She reads approximately a book a day but writes much slower than that.

3

Squeekie and Bingo

Samantha Coons

Squeekie perched on the catwalk above the counter, tail twitching back and forth.

A three year old human stared dolefully up at him, a thumb stuck into their mouth.

He should go down, he really should. He was the bookstore cat, and it was his job to greet all the humans no matter how small and sticky they were.

But it had been a trying day, one of those days when all the humans seemed to have nothing better to do than come into the store all day long and chase him around. He had been picked up more times than he could count. And the number of treats in compensation was truly pitiful.

Just when he thought the day was over, when the sky outside darkened and Mother prepared to leave, a harried mother and her child ran through the door. The mother made human noises at Mother very quickly and Mother nodded before leading her off to another part of the store. She left the child sitting at the counter.

The toddler reached a pudgy hand up and made grabby motions.

"Kitty," it squeaked in human, a poor imitation of Squeekie himself.

"Not right now thank you," Squeekie said politely.

The toddler giggled. Sometimes Squeekie wondered how smart humans could even be. Sure they made a lot of tasty things, and soft beds, but they never seemed to understand him properly. Kind of like kittens but with less pointy bits.

"No," Squeekie repeated slowly.

The toddler stood on tiptoe, reaching maybe two inches higher but still falling short of touching Squeekie by at least a foot.

Squeekie sighed and stretched his back legs before he pounced down onto the counter. The toddler wasted no time in grabbing Squeekie fur in its best estimation of a pet.

It wasn't too bad. Not as nice as adult's petting him, but the child wasn't rough and its hands weren't sticky enough to catch on his fur so he endured it. His tail still twitched, but he could hardly control that, now could he?

The child stopped with a handful of fur in its small fist. It pulled out the thumb from its mouth and pointed up at the catwalk.

"Hi kitty," it said in its small shrill voice.

Squeekie was surprised. They were between fosters, so only he and Annika remained in the bookstore, and Annika almost always hid in one of her small dark corners. Squeekie couldn't believe she would come out to see a child after avoiding humanity all day.

"Wat's 'kitty'?" an unfamiliar voice quirked from the catwalk.

Squeekie scrambled around, tearing himself from the child's grasp. An intruder? In his bookstore? Not on his watch. He would protect his home and this pudgy little human with his life.

He crouched low, preparing to lunge.

It was not a skunk, as he had thought. Skunks gave him no end of trouble, prancing around outside the door at night and being smelly. It was not even a possum nor a strange cat from outside the glass door.

In fact, Squeekie had no idea what it was. He checked his pounce, wary of the new creature.

It was about his size, and brown scales covered its whole body. It had bright beady eyes and tiny white horns sticking out of its head. It tilted its head at Squeekie.

Footsteps approached from the backroom and Squeekie's attention wavered from the new creature for half a second. When he looked back it was gone.

Mother and the child's mother came back, the other mother making a lot of grateful human noises. She paid for one of those paper book things humans like so much and left, the toddler staring

Squeekie and Bingo

up where the creature had been while its mother led it away by the hand.

A few minutes after they left Mother turned off the lights and left herself, saying she would see me tomorrow as she shut the door.

Once she left I set off, leaping up the catwalks to search for the odd creature.

Annika spotted me as she pranced toward the kitchen.

"Squeekie," she called, "why are you running around? The humans are gone, it's dinnertime."

Squeekie paused right above her.

"Investigating," he said, before bouncing off.

Annika sniffed and continued on her way to the food bowl.

Squeekie stopped at one of the intersections on the wooden paths, putting his nose down to sniff at the paint. He caught a faint whiff of...strangeness. He followed it farther, creeping along so he didn't lose the scent or scare the creature away.

It led back around to the counter, becoming stronger as he stepped onto the top of the entrance. He wove around the old dusty chairs and an old display case.

Past the clutter a lone paper box, long forgotten, shuffled along the floor. Squeekie perked up and padded silently over, wiggling once before heaving himself onto the edge of the box. His paws landed on the thin edge and it upset, the creature yelping inside.

It blinked at him, a few old pieces of paper clutched in its claws.

"Excuse you," it huffed and set about straightening the crumpled sheets.

"Excuse *you*," Squeekie retorted, "you are trespassing in *my* bookstore."

The creature paused.

"Wat's a bookstore?" it asked.

Squeekie puffed himself up and raised his chin.

"A bookstore," he said patiently, "is a place where humans buy these things called 'books' that are a bunch of papers in a box shape, and where Mother has her talky nights with her 'book club' where humans gather to make noise about books."

The creature scratched its nose.

"So it's a sorta library," it said.

"What's a library?" Squeekie asked, deflating a bit.

"You know," it said, waddling out of the sideways box, "Humans keep books there and then they come ask a lotta questions. Or sit around and stare at the books."

Squeekie sat back.

"Sounds like a bookstore," he said.

The creature nodded.

"That's what I said," it began walking toward the chairs, "I live in a library. You can come see it if you want."

Squeekie only considered a moment before following the scaly thing toward one of fancier dusty chairs.

"I'm Squeekie the bookstore cat, by the way," he said as he caught up.

"Hmmm," the creature gave him a once-over, "yeah, you are a cat."

"I'm Bingo," the creature added.

It-or he, Squeekie supposed, set his papers down and nudged the chair over a few inches with his rump.

"Pardon the rudeness, uh, Bingo, but what are you?" Squeekie asked.

Bingo paused again, apparently thinking his answer through.

"Sorta a dragon," he answered, picking his papers up again and moving around the chair.

Squeekie was fairly certain dragons didn't exist, or at least the humans at book club didn't seem to think they did. But humans weren't very bright and Bingo wasn't anything Squeekie had ever met, so they were probably wrong.

Bingo waved him over. Squeekie went over to him before backing up in alarm, the hair on his shoulders standing high.

Between the chair legs was a window, but it wasn't a window. Squeekie could move to the side and it was gone. But facing it straight on it sat there, more or less rectangular and glowing at the edges. Through it he saw long bookshelf made of smooth, dark wood and the sun shining through large windows. He hopped away to peer down at the bookstore's windows. Still dark.

He ran back and stared again.

"How?" he whispered.

Squeekie and Bingo

Bingo shrugged.

"Itsa fancy door I found. It opens to different places on different days. I go through and find stuff for my nest and then go home."

Squeekie yowled as Bingo stepped across the threshold and stood in the light, waiting for him to follow. He took a step toward the small dragon then froze.

"Wait, will I be able to get back to the bookstore?" he asked.

Bingo nodded impatiently, folding his tiny arms.

"Door doesn't close until I close it."

Squeekie wasn't sure how much he trusted his new 'friend', but he was a cat, and there are sayings about curiosity and cats.

He stepped through, and quickly glanced back. The cinderblock wall of the bookstore still lay behind him. He sighed in relief.

Bingo was already waddling away. They were in some kind of vent, the 'door' facing a hole in the stone leading to the library. Bingo went instead to the left down the vent. It led to a little room, a good size for a cat or dragon (or at least a Bingo), and filled with junk. Bingo tucked the papers against the wall near a pile of mismatched clothes that might have been Bingo's bed. Beside it a bored looking skull wrapped in a scarf rested on a plush cushion.

"That's Rupert," Bingo said, patting the skull.

The skull said nothing.

"He's sleepy," Bingo said, waddling back toward the door.

Squeekie swore he heard someone grumbling behind him as he followed Bingo back toward the door and the open vent.

This time he headed out onto the bookshelves, Squeekie trailing behind him.

Squeekie's bookstore was a large building. Squeekie knew because people said it to Mother all the time. But this place completely dwarfed it. It extended to either side of them farther than Squeekie could run without taking a break or three. Which was pretty far for a cat his age, he thought proudly.

"What do they do with them all?" he said in awe, looking down at the books.

"Stare at them," Bingo answered confidently, "although one of the human girls that visits a lot tells me it's called 'reading'. And they learn when they read."

"Sounds like magic to me," Squeekie said.

"They do that too," Bingo nodded.

Squeekie didn't know what that meant but followed Bingo down to the library floor via a series of neatly stacked books by the back wall. Bingo led him down the stacks of books out into open area, mostly filled with tables and chairs, with one large circular desk sitting in the middle.

A man with long dark hair stood in the middle, holding up a large tome. He raised an eyebrow as they went past him.

"What's this?" he asked, frowning down at them.

"Itsa cat," Bingo said without pausing.

The man pinched the bridge of his nose and took a long breath.

"I can see that much," he said very slowly, "but why is it here?"

Bingo paused and thought. Squeekie noticed he had trouble doing both at the same time.

"He lives in bookstore," Bingo said.

The man grit his teeth and turned away from them. Bingo kept going.

"Who was that?" Squeekie asked.

"The librarian," Bingo answered, "he's grumpy but only because he doesn't have any friends. At least that's what people told me."

"How could he understand you so well?" Squeekie pressed. He had never before seen a human hold an actual conversation with a cat. They usually just made up the cat's half like the cat wasn't even speaking.

"Mmmm, he's pretty smart," Bingo said.

Squeekie let it go, guessing he wouldn't get much more of an answer out of the dragon.

They reached a table tucked away by one of the many front windows. Bingo scrambled up and Squeekie leapt after him.

A young woman sat at the table, leaning back slightly in her chair and staring out at the sky. She was very tall and her brown hair was cut short. Bingo patted her on the shoulder.

She looked around and set her chair down, smiling.

"Hi Bingo, new friend today?" she asked.

"Yes," he said, "New friend so double treats."

Squeekie and Bingo

She laughed and rummaged in the satchel sitting next to her on the table. She pulled out two large cookies, handing Bingo one and laying the other one down in front of Squeekie. He sniffed it, and it smelled nice, so he nibbled a bit. He swallowed and began going at it with a will.

Bingo finished his cookie before Squeekie was halfway through his. He made the same grabby motion as the toddler had in the store earlier.

"Sorry Bingo. You know I've gotten in trouble before for too many treats so I think one is enough for today."

Bingo pouted, his head flopping dramatically onto his shoulder.

"He feeds you," the girl pointed out. Squeekie guessed she meant the librarian.

Bingo was now halfway slumped over onto the table.

"But not sweets," he whined. He flopped completely over onto his side, staring as Squeekie finished the last of his cookie.

Squeekie privately agreed with Bingo, but the girl didn't seem impressed by Bingo's performance so he kept it to himself.

"Thank you for the cookie," he said politely. Humans liked polite when they could understand it.

"You're welcome," the girl said, ignoring the dragon rolling dramatically from side to side.

"You can understand me?" Squeekie asked.

She patted his head.

"It was a lucky guess," Bingo said as he straightened up.

"What's a lucky guess?" she asked.

Bingo waddled to her and patted her head.

"He thought you could speak cat," he said, "But you can't. Only I can."

The girl grimaced.

"Not me, sorry," she told Squeekie, "but I could tell you were being polite."

Squeekie smirked. Humans did like polite.

"Well, new friend must go now. Bring more treats tomorrow," Bingo jumped down to the ground.

Squeekie rubbed against the girl's shoulder before he hopped down after the dragon. She scratched behind his ears as he went.

Samantha Coons

She was quite intelligent for a human, Squeekie thought as he padded down the rows after Bingo. They passed the grumpy librarian again but he pretended not to notice them. They climbed up the stacks of books to the top of the bookshelves and crossed over toward Bingo's nest in the wall.

"Thank you for visiting Squeekie the Bookstore Cat," Bingo said, "Come back anytime, but bring your own cookie next time so I can have two."

They stopped at the hole in the wall.

"Oh," said Squeekie.

Bingo scratched his head.

"Did your bookstore have sand in it?" he asked.

A white sandy beach with waving palm trees now lay beyond the strange door, a cruise ship honking in the distance. The cinderblock wall was completely gone.

Squeekie was stranded.

"You brought this cat through a what?" the shocked librarian asked.

An hour had passed since they discovered the beach scene beyond Bingo's special door. Squeekie had been stunned for a split second then began yowling so loudly it rang throughout the entire library. Both the librarian and the cookie girl came running to see what was wrong. Bingo and the librarian had been talking in circles ever since as neither of them seemed to understand the other's way of speaking.

The cookie girl held Squeekie now, petting down his back as he whimpered.

Bingo tapped a scaly paw on the desk.

"Itsa fancy door. It's next to my nest."

The librarian took a deep breath.

"A fancy door that leads different places every time you use it?" he asked slowly.

Bingo considered this then nodded.

"Have you, *ever*, heard of a portal?" the librarian asked.

Bingo considered this as well and shook his head.

Squeekie and Bingo

"Of course not," the librarian muttered. He ran a hand through his long hair.

"Door's not supposed to change until I close it," Bingo said, climbing onto the book in front of the librarian, "Rupert must have done it while I got a cookie."

The librarian shot a glare at the girl when Bingo said cookie. She shrugged and kept petting Squeekie.

"So I can't go home?" Squeekie mewled. Bingo translated for him.

The librarian opened the small door on the desk and stepped out.

"Not necessarily," he said. He buzzed off down an aisle and disappeared from sight.

"We'll do whatever we can to get you home Squeekie," the girl said. She dug a hand into her bag and pulled out a cookie, breaking off a piece for Squeekie to take from her hand. Bingo rolled over on the book where he stood. The girl sighed and broke half of the cookie off for him.

"One and a half cookies," Bingo murmured under his breath, wolfing his half down in a matter of seconds. He picked the last few crumbs off his claws with his tongue and wrapped himself in the page of the book.

The librarian strode back with a small volume in one hand and saw Bingo. He went red in the face.

"Get out of that book this instant," he barked.

Bingo scuttled backward and fell onto the floor behind the desk. The librarian swept away the large tome and placed it carefully on the table in front of the girl.

"Can you get me home?" Squeekie squeaked.

The librarian raised an eyebrow but said nothing as he flipped open the small book. He turned his attention to the thin paper, brow wrinkled.

The girl shifted underneath him. She opened her mouth then closed it after a second. Squeekie guessed she wanted to ask too but was too afraid of the librarian. He couldn't blame her.

Bingo scaled up the girl's arm and perched on her shoulder.

"Whatchu find?" he asked the librarian, waving a paw at the book.

"An old book," the librarian said, staring down at the pages intently, "now hush."

Bingo blinked but stayed silent.

For a whole minute.

"What if it just looks like the portal is going to the wrong place?" he asked.

The librarian rubbed the bridge of his nose.

"Has that ever happened before?" he said in a deadly calm voice.

Bingo shook his head and grabbed onto a handful of the girl's hair to steady himself as she snorted.

The librarian went back to the book.

A moment later he laid the book in front of them on the desk.

"There, extradimensional re-calibration," he said.

"Extra...celebration?" Bingo repeated, or tried to repeat, "We shouldn't be celebrating, Squeekie is sad."

The librarian ignored him and spoke to Squeekie and the girl.

"The simplest way to fix the portal is to introduce an object from your world to the origin point of the portal, which should be somewhere on the wall behind it."

"You mean I have to give up my papers? But I just got them," Bingo whined.

The librarian shook his head.

"Paper might work but it's not specific enough to Squeekie's bookstore. If you use the paper there's no telling where the portal would lead. No, if you want to get him home, the safest way is to use part of Squeekie himself."

Squeekie yowled and curled up tighter in the girl's lap. Bingo scrambled down beside him and patted his head.

"Don't worry," he said, "We'll take something small. Like an ear."

The girl flicked Bingo away.

"I think it might be better to use some hair or a whisker," she said.

That sounded better to Squeekie but he still didn't want his hair or whiskers plucked out.

Squeekie and Bingo

"How about this?" he said, brushing a paw over his collar.

Bingo relayed the message. The librarian lifted Squeekie's chin and inspected the faded red, white, and blue fabric.

"I think that should work perfectly."

Once again Bingo and Squeekie approached the portal, still leading out onto the sandy beach.

The librarian and the girl were down at the base of the bookshelf, since they were not as nimble as a cat or dragon and couldn't climb up safely.

"Just stick your paw onto the wall behind the portal and feel around until the destination changes," the librarian called up to Bingo.

"Good luck," the girl added.

Bingo stuck his clawed fist against the wall behind the beach scene, clutching the collar tight. He jerked his arm up and down the wall, looking more than a little silly and not affecting the portal at all.

"Maybe try really high up and really low down," Squeekie said, a little desperately.

Bingo went up on his tiptoes to where wall met ceiling. Nothing happened.

He crouched down and reached to where the wall met the floor and the beach swirled away into a stack of books on a table, lit up by the orange glow of sunrise.

"Got it," Squeekie trilled. He yowled in delight.

Bingo pulled his hand out, the collar gone.

"We got it," he yelled down to the humans.

The girl cheered.

"Go home Squeekie," she cried.

He didn't need telling twice. He stepped through the portal.

And he was home.

He pounced on his favorite cat bed and smushed his face into the familiar scent of cat and book.

Bingo trailed after him; the portal still open behind him.

"It was good to meet you, Squeekie the Bookstore Cat," he said. He laid a lumpy looking treat down at Squeekie's front paws, "this is from my personal cookie stash. Since I almost got you stuck in my library."

Squeekie was touched despite himself. He purred.

"Visit again sometime and I'll introduce to my humans," he told Bingo, "I bet they'd like to meet a dragon."

"Do they have cookies?" Bingo asked.

Squeekie laughed and nodded.

"Okay then," Bingo said. He waved and waddled through the portal, which closed with a slurp once the end of his tail disappeared.

Squeekie sighed and examined the 'cookie'. He leaned down to sniff it.

"Hey," came a shrill voice from the ground, "where have you been all night? And why do I smell food?"

"Annika," Squeekie yelled, launching himself down at her.

Once she recovered from his shower of affection, he told her all about his adventures.

She didn't believe most of it, but Squeekie still offered her half of the cookie.

It was delicious.

Squeekie and Bingo

AUTHOR BIOGRAPHY

Samantha Coons writes words more or less competently. She edited this book and apologizes for any mistakes.

Squeekie the Bookstore Cat

4

The Perfect Match

Carrie Jacobs

"There's a new rescue cat coming." Annika said, watching the parking lot from her perch high atop a mountain of books near the window.

Squeekie stretched and yawned as he climbed out of his warm and cozy cat bed. He licked his paws and watched as the rescue volunteer brought the cat carrier into the store and put the newest arrival into the big cage at the front of the store.

The new cat hunkered in the back corner, warily surveying the space, her white fur poofed up to warn everyone to stay away.

Squeekie waited until the volunteer left and the store was quiet before padding over to the cage. "*Anna Karenina.*"

"That's not my name," the new cat hissed.

"Sorry. I'm getting ahead of myself. I'm Squeekie. This is my home. Welcome."

"Welcome? I'm in prison."

"You'll be allowed out to roam shortly. I know this is hard for you."

The new cat yowled at the top of her lungs. "You don't know anything!"

Squeekie recognized the defensive fear, and wasn't offended. He used his calming voice. "I know it won't be long until you find your forever home. Until then, you'll be living here in the bookstore with us. Annika's up there," he nodded in her direction. "This is her home, too. What's your name?"

"Lexi. Why did you call me Anna?"

"*Anna Karenina*. It's not a name. Well, it is, but... it's a book. By Leo Tolstoy."

"What does that have to do with me?"

Annika huffed an annoyed sigh. "Squeekie has a *special gift*." Sarcasm dripped from her words. "When a new cat comes in, he assigns them a book."

Squeekie interrupted. "I don't assign the book."

Annika continued as though he hadn't spoken. "Then he keeps an eye out because he also assigned that book to the human who will take you to your forever home or something. Blah, blah, blah."

"That's not exactly how it works."

Lexi's whiskers furrowed in confusion. She perked her ears forward. "How *does* it work?"

Just then a customer came in and rattled a container of treats. A rescue kitten raced from the back of the store toward the sound. "Hi," he yelled as he zoomed past the cage and rubbed against the treat-bearing customer.

The customer fed the kitten a treat. Annika looked on with disdain. "That's Milo."

"Ooooh, aren't you a cutie?" The customer was leaning down, scratching Milo's head.

A store employee leaned on the counter. "He's getting his forever home today."

Squeekie abandoned his treat. "What? That can't be right."

"What's the matter?" Annika asked.

Squeekie ran over to her and lowered his voice so Milo couldn't hear. "His forever person hasn't been in yet."

"Apparently they have." Annika jumped up to a higher level of books and curled up for another nap. "You must have missed them."

Squeekie went to hide at the back of the store so he could gather his thoughts. He didn't miss them. He couldn't have. He hadn't ever missed one.

Later that afternoon, an excited family came in, loaded Milo into an expensive cat carrier, chatted for a few minutes, then took Milo out the door.

"Squeekie, relax. It'll be fine."

The Perfect Match

"I'm sure you're right." The family seemed nice enough. Maybe... maybe it would be okay.

Lexi inched closer to the front of the cage. "Why are you worried?"

"I know it's hard to understand," Squeekie said, "but Milo was supposed to go to a forever home with someone looking for John Grisham books. They're a really nice family. I've seen them lots of times. But it's not the perfect match." He sighed.

Annika chimed in, "Squeekie's the resident idealist."

Several days went by. Squeekie watched and listened, but no one asked for *Anna Karenina*. Lexi was let out of kitty prison to explore the store, and everything was back to normal. Until Tuesday afternoon, when an apologetic and upset woman came in the door... with Milo.

As soon as she opened the cat carrier, Milo darted up onto the counter and jumped up, up, up, until he reached the catwalk and ran along the bookshelves until he found a hiding place in a far corner.

"What happened?"

"Squeekie, it was awful." Milo wailed. He held up his back paw, revealing a long scratch. Thankfully, it wasn't deep. "Bugsy – their big, fat, mean jerk of a cat – hated me. He hissed at me and smacked me and tried to bite me. I stayed out of his way, but he cornered me at the food dish this morning and scratched me. And the worst thing? They let the littlest human change my name."

"To what?"

"Peanut Butter!"

Squeekie made a face. That was a terrible forever name. "Get some rest, Milo." Then he went on his rounds of the store, took a nap of his own, and went off in search of a snack.

"John Grisham."

The words, spoken at the front counter, made Squeekie's ears perk up. He gracefully made his way to the floor, then dashed to the front.

A new customer was at the counter, looking at a piece of paper. "We already have *The Reckoning, The Firm*, and *A Time to Kill*. My wife asked me to stop here and see if you had any more of his books."

"Tons. Right this way." The employee led him to a big section of John Grisham books.

While he browsed, Squeekie inched closer.

"Hey, little buddy." The man hunkered down.

Squeekie rewarded him with a "Meow!" followed by loud purrs and a rub against his knee. A moment later, he sprinted away.

"Milo! Milo, that's him."

Wary, Milo shook his head.

"Just take a look, okay? I think this is your forever human."

Milo followed Squeekie to the floor. Squeekie waited around the corner while Milo cautiously approached the man.

"Wow, another kitty?" He bent down again, this time to scratch Milo's head. "Ooh, you're a cutie. My wife would just love you."

"He's available for adoption," an employee said.

The man's eyebrows rose. "Really?" He stood and carried his armload of John Grisham books to the counter, where he was educated about Castaway Critters and the adoptable cats in the store.

Squeekie watched as he paid for his books and looked around for Milo before he left. He felt it in his gut. That was Milo's forever human. His perfect match. Squeekie just knew it!

Milo wasn't convinced. Until the next day, when they overheard the humans in the store talking about Milo getting another application.

Lexi asked, "What does that mean?"

"When a human wants to take you to your forever home, they have to fill out an application to make sure it's a good home."

"We don't even know if that's him," Milo grumbled.

Squeekie could barely contain his excitement. "It is. It has to be."

"Why haven't I gotten an application yet?" Lexi wondered out loud.

"Because your perfect match hasn't come in yet. But they will."

Several days later, they cheered as the John Grisham guy came in with his wife and took Milo to his forever home – for real this time.

"Soon," Squeekie said to Lexi.

The Perfect Match

Another week passed before a teenage girl and her mom came into the store. "Hi. We're looking to see if you happen to have a copy of *Anna Karenina*."

Squeekie watched Lexi's ears perk up and followed her as she trotted toward the classics.

"This looks boring," the girl said.

"It's full of angst and drama. Pretend it's just one super long post online, and you'll love it," the mother joked.

The girl rolled her eyes. "Whatever. Oh, hey." She plopped down onto the floor and crossed her legs. "Hi, kitty."

Lexi inched over, stretched out to sniff the girl's fingertips, then rubbed her head against her hand.

Squeekie saw tears in the girl's eyes, and a loving look on the mom's face.

"You're so pretty. My kitty just passed away," the girl whispered to Lexi.

Lexi climbed into her lap. Purring, she leaned up and nudged her chin.

Squeekie heard a sniffle and glanced over at Annika. "Are you cry-"

"No! Shut your face," Annika hissed, wiping her eyes.

A few days later, Lexi was safely nestled into a new cat carrier, on her way to her new forever home.

That afternoon, a volunteer from the rescue brought in a new cat.

Squeekie sighed and smacked his forehead with his paw.

"What?" Annika asked.

"I knew it was bound to happen sooner or later."

"What?"

"*Fifty Shades*. This cat's book is *Fifty Shades*."

Annika made a barfing noise, then guffawed loudly.

Squeekie wailed, "I've told you a million times, I do not assign the books!"

Carrie Jacobs

AUTHOR BIOGRAPHY

Carrie Jacobs began her writing career at age three, when, still lacking the dexterity to form recognizable letters, she dictated a riveting tale to her transcriptionist, AKA Mom. "A Frog Named Tog" rocketed to #1 in the family, but did not garner international acclaim. It did, however, serve as an early clue that writing would be a lifelong journey.

Since then, she spent approximately fifteen years as a columnist for a local weekly newspaper, writing "slice of life" type articles. She also frequently write articles for a local non-profit. Carrie has won two first-place awards through Pennwriters.

She loves writing contemporary romance novels, and writes short stories in any genre imaginable, including the weird and creepy. Her settings are many places she's visited and her hometown, all thrown into a blender and poured out into the place she would most love to live. Her characters are people she knows, would like to know, or would like to avoid.

Carrie lives in beautiful central Pennsylvania with her family and spoiled pets.

Connect with her on Facebook at facebook.com/writercarriejacobs, on Twitter at @carrieinpa or on her website at carrieajacobs.com.

5

Squeekie Goes to the Horse Barn

Kristian Beverly

Squeekie never suspected to open his eyes and find himself *here*. Not that it was a bad here.

The best adventures happen not only by accident but with the best intentions. Those two ideas equaled the root of all of Squeekie's decisions. He believed, so he did.

The woman didn't know that he'd snuck his way onto the horse trailer. He'd heard it drive into the parking lot, and he'd stared at the long contraption through the window.

What a fun house they've bought for me, Squeekie thought.

He'd yearned for a vacation for a while now. Just a nice getaway with plenty of catnip and treats. He'd called for Annika to glance at the trailer, but the fluffy cat huffed and trotted away. She'd told him that his exploring would land him in trouble. No, she didn't say it that way. It'd come out as she would love to watch him land in trouble but that she had no desire of going out to see it happen.

He sat in the spot he wasn't supposed to and watched the human carry a box large enough for him and Annika to lay in without them touching each other. She only liked to be touched when treats were involved and since he wanted them the same amount as her, playing didn't happen much.

Squeekie knew he'd have just one chance to see his fun house. The box was large enough that he could slip out without her seeing him. Without any of his humans seeing him.

He gave one large yowl at the window before hopping down and trotting to the door. One chance.

Annika watched from the closest bookcase. She shook her head at him and mumbled just loud enough for him to hear, "You will say I told you so. And you will let me have your treats after you get back."

Squeekie ignored her as the woman opened the door and he slipped out as it was about to close. The grass looked particularly tempting today, but he had more important things to learn about. The footing moved beneath his paws, some of the gravel pieces getting in between his toes. He flicked his ears back as he crouched towards the trailer. His mother had mentioned it. About the maneuvering capabilities of the driver and how well she parked it.

Which solidified to Squeekie that it was for him. He turned his ears forward as a different sound emerged from the metal slits. It was a grand thing, with legs longer than humans and a head the size of him.

"What are you?" he marveled.

"I am a horse," Horse said. "And I am ready to go home."

Squeekie moved closer to the trailer. Disappointment swept through him. This wasn't for him after all. "Where is home?"

"A place with other horses. She said she'd give me peppermints and a bath because I jumped well today. She always gives me treats, but today they'll be extra special because she was so happy. I won her books that she already owned."

Squeekie cocked his head. Peppermint treats had to taste well if the horse would jump for them.

"Will she give me treats?" Squeekie asked.

The horse turned its head at looked at Squeekie. "No, but she does give the barn cats things that they make much noise about."

That's all Squeekie needed to hear. He ran underneath the trailer before getting to the other side, jumping onto the wheels, and slipping through the lowest opening. He sneezed at the hay and maneuvered himself so that he perched on an unused bale.

Horse sniffed him before nibbling on hay. Squeekie tried a piece but it tasted too bland for his taste buds.

Soon, footsteps caught his attention and excitement combed through his body. He was going away on an adventure! The trailer lurched forward, causing the cat to grip the bale with his nails.

Squeekie Goes to the Horse Barn

How long was the trailer ride? Squeekie didn't know nor did Horse. He just adjusted his hold depending on the turn the truck made. The air swooshed around him, sending new smells through his nose. This alone was an adventure and Squeekie hadn't even gotten to his actual destination yet.

Horse started stomping, his body making the trailer sway.

Squeekie glared at his tall friend. "Can you stop?"

Horse paused, turning his large head towards Squeekie. "But we're home!"

Squeekie blinked and looked out through the slit. The world had stopped, and outside he saw lots of grass and white fences and a large white weather barn.

He needed to slip out before the girl found him. He said goodbye to Horse and wiggled out of the trailer. He started his way to the barn.

Squeekie padded down the barn aisle, the smell of hay, horse, and soap filling his nose. What were the rules here? The horses stood in stalls or walked around paddocks, the lines of where they were and weren't supposed to explore clearly marked. At the bookstore, stealing human food wasn't allowed. It was marked with a type of door. He also knew that he wasn't *supposed* to stick his head out of the door to nibble on grass. It was marked by a slick feeling under his feet. That's how he'd landed himself in an unfamiliar place.

But he could smell the other cats. *And they were everywhere.* Up and down the aisle. Above, on the support beams. *Like my cat walk at home, just narrower*, he thought. *I'll have to try that out later.* The smell of them lingered even on the horses themselves. Their noses smelled of humans the same way as nice foster cats did. As if humans rubbed their scent on their fur because of their great big hearts.

He sat on his haunches, tail flicking back and forth. Where was he supposed to sleep? Where was his plushy and outlandish bed? Annika loved to laugh at his plushy throne, but Squeekie loved its softness. He glanced around.

Where were the other cats?

He trotted out to the door, glancing down at the rain falling out of the sky.

He yowled.

No response.

He yowled louder.

No response.

He took in the largest breath he could and started to yowl⸺

"Don't you dare. "

Squeekie jumped. A cat had landed right next to him. It wasn't fluffy, but had plushy white fur and a circle of brown on its head. The yellow eyes narrowed at him and its tail flicked from side to side. Annika and this cat would get along well.

The cat stretched to sniff Squeekie. It chuckled and looked Squeekie down. "You *so* do not belong here."

Squeekie huffed. "Do so. I came for treats."

The cat cocked its head. "A treat? Why'd you travel for treats when you could just live here and eat all types of things? And never have humans bother you unless you want them to bother you."

Squeekie sat down. "The treats humans give you."

The cat laughed and rolled on the floor, his fur soaking up dirt and hay.

Squeekie ignored the laugher. Treats probably had different names in different areas. Some of the cats that'd come into the bookstore didn't even know what a treat was.

"I'm Squeekie," he said.

The cat stopped laughing and stood up, shaking its fur. Not that it'd helped much.

"I don't bother to learn a new cat's name until it's been here for a month," the cat said. "But call me Bit."

Squeekie scoffed at that. Some cats stayed at the store for a day or two but he always made it a mission to know who a cat was.

"How'd you get that name?" Squeekie asked.

"I was found in a box with horse bits," Bit said.

The cat was already turning, sinking low as if it was about to launch off.

And it did. Squeekie watched as the cat jump onto the table and scraped up to the wood beam.

Squeekie Goes to the Horse Barn

While a month long seemed like too long of an adventure, he could surely last a night. Easily.

He crouched down and launched himself up to follow Bit. Squeekie landed on the table before jumping again to hit the rafter. Bit looked back at him before stepping away.

"So what do you do here?" Squeekie asked.

Bit sat down on his haunches and watched Squeekie scramble to get upright.

Bit gave a toothy smile. "I search for mice. Horses are fun to watch. I wander where I want and show back up when I feel like."

Squeekie cocked his head. "So—the humans don't let you in their house?"

Bit looked taken aback. "Why would I ever want to do that? They live behind doors, and I could never ever do that."

Squeekie shook his head. "But fluffy beds that—"

Bit started to walk across the rafters and Squeekie followed. Bit walked with such confidence, his tail swishing back and forth. Squeekie told himself to not look down because the fall here would probably hurt him.

Bit trotted to the other side of the barn and paused. "Fluffy things? No thank you. When it's warm the grass feels wonderful to sleep on. And the horses let me lounge on their backs."

Squeekie stared in horror. He loved to munch on grass, but to sleep on it instead of a bed? And he loved to sleep in the bookstore. He liked the doors for keeping away the smelly skunk and the loud groundhog. Or the bees. He particularly didn't love the sound of bumblebees.

Squeekie needed to go home. It crossed his mind for a brief second. He needed to concentrate on where he put his feet so he didn't fall off.

Bit had already dropped down into a stall with a large mound of hay. Squeekie followed him and sneezed. He sniffed at the blades again.

"Kitty! *Kitties.*" The girl's voice rang.

Squeekie didn't move. He glanced out of the stall and saw a girl walking into the barn. A parade of cats followed her. *That's where they were this whole time*, Squeekie thought.

Everything smelled of horse and rain. He scratched at his neck. Itchy.

The girl had a cupful of regular food. Where were the treats?

She made several piles of the food and each cat went to a pile. Squeekie listened to the purrs. The girl patted Bit and walked out of the barn.

He saw movement behind him and jumped on it. At least mice where the same no matter where he was.

After yowling to show the world he had successfully captured a mouse, Squeekie found Bit again.

He trotted out of the stall before pausing at Horse's stall. The horse was black from being wet and he licked his lips. Squeekie stretched before sitting down.

"Didn't you mention treats?" Squeekie asked.

Bit sat down beside Squeekie and gave him a smug look. "Yes. Please tell the cat about treats."

Horse looked down at Squeekie and blew out a long breath. Squeekie breathed in the hay and peppermint smell and grew annoyed. This was a disaster of a vacation. He had yet to have treats and had no comfy bed.

Horse said, "Didn't she give you guys the nightly food?"

Squeekie sighed. It was just regular food, not special food. He said thank you to Horse and sat down in the aisle. The other cats had disappeared, so Squeekie was left only with Bit.

"I told you that this isn't the place for you," Bit said. "Even though I hope you had fun climbing. It's my favorite part. If the weather wasn't so bad I would show you the woods. But rain makes mud and mud is unpleasant if you're—well—"

Squeekie finished the sentence for him. "—If you aren't used to it."

Bit nodded and slashed his tail. "You did a good job catching the mouse."

Squeekie nodded. "Thank you."

"Mice aren't good for horses. They aren't good for us when people poison them."

Squeekie stood up and moved towards the mouth of the barn. Maybe this vacation wasn't a disaster. Just different and unique.

Squeekie Goes to the Horse Barn

He and Bit climbed into Horse's stall. Squeekie slept at the horse's feet and Bit climbed upon his back.

In the morning the light shone through the stall doors and Squeekie cracked open an eye.

The girl!

He stepped out into the aisle of the barn and watched her. She threw bales into each stall and the horses nickered in response. It reminded Squeekie of the parade of cats just without a herd being able to follow the girl.

The girl turned to him and her eyes widened. "You're Squeekie."

Squeekie cocked his head and meowed.

The girl laughed. "Your mom has you on every online platform trying to find you!"

It didn't take long before the girl picked him up and placed him in a cat carrier. He did get a chance to say goodbye to his friends before he had a feeling that he wouldn't see them again.

The girl put him into her truck and Squeekie started the journey home. He liked it better inside a car than the trailer.

He found himself in kitty jail when he returned. Annika laughed at the dirty state he was in, but Squeekie said he would let her have his treats. For a few days. Not forever. But at least he had his fluffy bed.

Kristian Beverly

AUTHOR BIOGRAPHY

Kristian Beverly loves to write and has been writing her whole life. Before being able to write, she illustrated her stories but now write short fiction and novels. When not writing, Kristian can be found on the back of a horse, creating art, or reading.

6

Squeekie and the Lost Human

Katie Twigg

"Let me go!" a voice shrieks. Squeekie's ears prick up at the harsh sound.

"Please let me go! I need to find my human!" Squeekie raises his head. The voice isn't familiar. It definitely doesn't belong to any cat in the store. Curious, he decides to investigate. Squeekie jumps from the table and then heads to where the unknown voice is still yelling.

At the counter Squeekie finds a woman talking with his mother. He recognizes her as a frequent visitor but is more interested in the cat carrier at her feet. He trots over to it deciding that it must be his now and he settles in, finally turning his attention to their conversation.

"I would keep him at home but my niece is visiting and she's allergic to cats," the other lady says. "I had my husband ask around the neighborhood but no one recognized him."

"How did you catch him?" Michelle asks.

"We didn't try to. I opened our back door to take the garbage out and he just ran in."

They both turn to look at the cat cage. Inside, Squeekie sees a pouting cat, curled up in HIS bed. He is almost entirely black with bright yellow eyes. A single white spot is centered on his nose and mouth. Making him look like he just stuck his nose in ice cream.

Noticing them staring, the cat jumps up and starts to yell again. "Let me out of here! My human is lost! I need to find her!"

Squeekie's mother shakes her head, "He looks well fed. I doubt he's a stray."

"That's what we were thinking."

The cat, realizing his cries are being ignored, slumps back into the bed. Squeekie huffs. *Of course, he has to lay in MY bed.*

"Are you sure this is alright?" the lady asks. "Him staying here for now."

"Of course."

"I'll be back this evening to get him as soon as I take my niece home."

"We close at eight."

"I'll be back before then."

Suddenly, the carrier gets lifted up. Squeekie yells in surprise and jumps to the floor.

"Squeekie!" the lady exclaims. "When did you get in there?" She laughs and gives him a much-too-quick pat, leaving him dissatisfied.

The lady heads to the door saying over her shoulder, "Thank you so much, Michelle."

After the ding from the door, Squeekie jumps onto the counter, knowing that now is the perfect time for pets.

Michelle obliges and rubs his head. "Do you see our new guest, Squeekie? He's scared so be nice to him." Then she walks away.

Squeekie turns to the cage. The small cat watches him with sad eyes.

Squeekie calls out, "What's wrong?"

"I lost my human."

"Oh no," Squeekie says. He couldn't imagine ever losing his humans. "How did you lose her?"

"She kept walking in and out of the big door today. I wanted to know what she was doing so I went out when she wasn't paying attention. But then I saw a bushy tailed rodent that runs in the trees and I thought that it would play with me. I tried to chase it but it didn't want to play and ran away. Then I didn't know where I was. And my person was not with me."

Squeekie thinks about what to do. "What's your name?"

"Binx"

"I'm Squeekie. Don't worry Binx. I'll find your human."

"Really?"

"Yep," Squeekie smiles. He had been to the Outside several times before. He hadn't gone very far but it couldn't be too much bigger than Home. Could it? "You just stay there. I'll be back with your human soon."

"Squeekie?" Binx calls out. Squeekie turns back to him. "My mama has purple hair. Maybe that will help you find her."

"Purple hair."

"And please find her fast. I miss her so much." He looks down at his paws.

Squeekie nods. *The first step*, he thinks, *is to get to the Outside*.

Squeekie walks into the entrance way, noticing Annika sitting up high next to the books on display. Her eyes are closed but Squeekie knows that she isn't sleeping. Her tail is hanging off the counter, swishing back and forth.

"Hi Annika," he says.

With her eyes still closed she replies, "Squeekie."

"Why are you sitting there?"

"The humans built too many scratching posts on the table and now I can't sit in my spot."

"Scratching posts? You mean the stacks of books."

"Call them what you want. They keep my claws sharp and ready for the humans who try to pick me up."

Squeekie just shakes his head. Annika is always very strange to him. He couldn't understand her dislike of attention. *Pets are the No.2 best thing in the world*, he thinks. *Treats are the No.1.*

Squeekie hears footsteps on stones coming up to the door. His chance was coming.

Annika opens her eyes just as Squeekie creeps up to the door, hiding behind the bookcase to the right of the door. Knowing him well enough to assume he's going to the Outside, she just asks, "Where are you off to?"

He smiles back at her. "I'm going on an adventure!" he cheers.

The front door dings as a human walks in. Squeekie sprints past their feet onto the cold stones outside Home.

He pauses for a moment, listening for the exclamations that typically follow when he goes to the Outside. But as the door swings closed, all he hears is, "Hello, let me know if I can help you with—".

Success! Now, step number two. Find Binx's human.

Katie Twigg

Squeekie looks around admiring the marvels of the Outside. The sky looks so much bluer without looking through a window. The loud things (he thinks they are called cars) sound so much louder as they zoom by. The trains (as Bob the bookstore ghost calls them) look bigger.

Squeekie heads towards the black ground, trying to get an idea of where to start looking. Then he notices a tree. But it's a very weird looking tree. It's tall like a tree. It's brown like a tree. But has no leaves like a tree. Instead there's black string, really high up connecting the trees together. *Is this even a tree?* Even more strange, there's a piece of paper on the tree. MISSING it says along the top, with seven numbers along the bottom, and in the middle a picture of...*Binx!*

Squeekie looks round, thinking someone must have put this here. Maybe Binx's human. Then he notices a lady with short purple hair up the hill from him. She's holding a bunch of papers and putting one on another weird tree.

Purple hair! That must be her! She has to be Binx's human!

Squeekie runs up to her as fast as he can calling out, "Hey! Hey miss!"

The purple-haired lady glances around in confusion before finally seeing Squeekie. "What—?" She shakes her head, her eyes wide with surprise.

Squeekie stops in front of her, "Are you Binx's human?"

"Hey there little guy." She kneels down and pets his head. "What are you doing out here? It's dangerous this close to the road."

Squeekie shakes off the urge to get petted. *There are more important things to deal with right now.* He leans away from her hand, "I know where your baby is. Where Binx is. He's at Home. You need to come back to Home with me right now."

"I wonder where you came from. Maybe someone is missing you. I know I'm missing my kitty."

"He isn't missing! He's right over there!" Squeekie runs down the hill towards Home, stopping only when he realizes that she isn't following. "Come on!" Squeekie yells back to her.

She just stares at him with furrowed eyebrows. "Where are you going?"

Squeekie and the Lost Human

"To Home. Where Binx is. Now come on!"

He takes a couple more steps in the direction of Home and looks back at her.

"Do you—" she trails off, thinking. "Do you want me to follow you?"

"Yes! What else do you think I'm trying to say." Squeekie takes another few steps and looks at her.

"You do, don't you." She says almost to herself. She takes a small step forward. And then another. And another.

"Finally!" Squeekie yells. He makes his way towards Home again, without stopping this time. "Hurry up."

"I'm coming, I'm coming," she says, following him.

Once at the door Squeekie finds her almost caught up to him.

"Is this where you live?" she asks.

Squeekie paws at the door, "Open the door. Your cat is inside. Come on. Hurry."

She reaches down and picks him up before going inside.

"Hello, let me know if I can help you with anything." Michelle says from her chair.

The purple-haired lady goes to the counter. "Uh, yeah. Is this your cat?"

"Yes, that's Squeekie. He lives here in the store."

"I actually just found him outside. Along the road."

"What?" Michelle comes to the counter. "He was outside?"

"Yeah, I guess he must have gotten out somehow."

She turns to Squeekie, "Bad Squeekie! You know you aren't allowed out. Something could have happened to you."

"But I was just trying to help Binx," he whines.

"Well I'm glad nothing bad happened." The purple-haired lady sets Squeekie on the counter. "I need to get going."

"Thank you so much for bringing Squeekie back."

"It's no problem." She glances around. "This is a really nice store. I might come back some other day." She pats Squeekie on the head. "It was nice meeting you Squeekie."

"Thanks again." Michelle says.

The purple-haired lady just smiles as she steps away from the counter, intending to leave.

"Wait, you can't leave. Your baby is right over there. Stop!" Squeekie looks to the cage to see Binx asleep on HIS bed. "Binx wake up. Your human is here. I found your human!"

Binx opens his eyes, "Mama?" he asks, his voice quiet as he looks around. When his eyes fall on her he jumps from the bed and yells out, "Mama! I'm over here! Don't leave! I'm right here."

The purple-haired lady stops in her tracks. "Binx?" she says under her breath before turning around. Her eyes brighten as soon as she sees the small cat. "Binx!" she exclaims.

She rushes towards the cage as Binx yells "Mama! Mama! Mama!" The lady yanks open the doors and pulls Binx into her arms.

Squeekie grins as he sees the happy tears rolling down the purple-haired lady's cheeks as she snuggles into Binx's fur.

"Is that your cat?" Michelle asks.

The purple-haired lady lifts her head to wipe her tears up with her sleeve. She takes in a couple breathes before turning to Michelle and answering, "Yes".

She keeps Binx pulled tight against her and never stops scratching behind his ear. Squeekie could hear his satisfied purring. "We just moved into the neighborhood up the hill. I was moving some boxes into the house when he got out. I saw him go after a squirrel and then he was gone. I was so worried."

"I'm glad you have him back," Michelle says.

The purple-haired lady smiles and kisses Binx on the head.

Binx grins at Squeekie. "Thank you Squeekie. You found my human!"

"You're welcome," Squeekie smiles back. "Just try not to lose your human again."

"I won't."

"Thank you Squeekie," the purple-haired lady says, patting him on the head "You're amazing."

"Yes, I am," he says as he pushes against her hand. "And you can pay me with pets."

Squeekie and the Lost Human

AUTHOR BIOGRAPHY

Katie is from Lemoyne, Pennsylvania but is currently living in State College as she attends Penn State University. She is a senior, majoring in Digital and Print Journalism with minors in both English and Planetary Science & Astronomy. In the 2018 fall semester, she began an internship with the communications office of the Eberly College of Science within Penn State. This internship has given her the opportunity to write several pieces that have been published on Eberly's website along with Penn State News. This opportunity is the first step towards the career she hopes to someday have as a science writer.

Katie is an avid animal lover who works part-time in a boarding kennel where she gets to play with many different cats and dogs. At home, she loves to spend time with her boyfriend and their pets: two cats (Peaches and Perceus), a rat (Reina), a mouse (Cream), and a chinchilla (ChinChin). In her free time, she likes to read from her ever-growing collection of books that is currently over 1,100.

Katie was previously employed at Cupboard Maker Books for over two years. Those days were filled with passionate book discussions, adoring cats, and tons of fun. She still loves to visit the store, the cats, and everyone there as often as she can.

Squeekie the Bookstore Cat

7

My Distant Love

Heidi Hormel

This is unacceptable. I've allowed the one who insists he is the Double Fanged Terror (who is really the Annoying One) to inhabit my household, but I will NOT allow *him* to reside here. The other cat ... the Annika ... she is nothing.

I am the Feline Overlord, with my sleek Siamese seal coat, and I decide what happens here. No matter that *he* is Master of the Way of the Beloved Kitty, I will keep all of The Laps, even from fluffy and allegedly Siamese Annoying One — the one who learned the Way of the Beloved Kitty from *him* — Obi-Squeekie-wan. In the past, I had to share laps with the Annoying One, but not now. If I continue to allow him to share, then I must share with Obi-Squeekie-wan and that will not happen, despite the training I've had in the Way of the Beloved Kitty.

But maybe he is not as great as I remembered because the Annika has certainly not found the path of the Beloved Kitty, and she has been with *him* since ... well, the time that we had to part ways when I came here.

The only reason Obi-Squeekie-wan and the Annika were here was that the Book Store – the place from where all cats come —was being "painted." That's what the human said, but then they got boring, so I walked away. My tail high so the Annika could tell that I was the most important feline here.

Now, was the time for me to act. The Annoying One would be distracted by the other cats, which gave me ample time to win back and keep all of The Laps. I went to my thinking place in the window between the glass that was as warm as the fire and the slats that could be put up and down. The heat, though, made me sleepy, so I napped and dreamed of getting back all The Laps.

Betsi. Betsi. My special name was not being said by Her of the Laps. Who else called me that? Then I recognized it was Obi-Squeekie-wan. I started awake; he was beside me.

"Me-rowr," he said, telling me that he'd been surprised to see me and I looked well.

I wanted to preen at the complement but reminded myself that we had parted long ago and far away. I was no longer the feline who hung on his every word and expected to share a cat bed. I was the Feline Overlord. I ruled this house.

"Hiss," I responded, reminding him that he was just a guest and only because I allowed him to be.

Smack came the response and not from Obi-Squeekie-wan. It was the Annika. Fluffly like the Annoying One but with an attitude that said this was her perch and Obi-Squeekie-wan was hers.

"Grrl," I responded with a one-two paw to the ear, followed by a leap from the window and into a space that her wide girth wouldn't allow her. Hah! I was sleek, mean, and lean. Except my whole body didn't fit.

"Er-rowr," said the Annoying One, telling me he was already hiding there – obviously.

"Meow," I told him that he was supposed to be the Double Fanged Terror, so why was he hiding?

The Annika, he answered in a whining hiss.

"Ee-ow," laughed the Annika at my hindquarters.

I was the Feline Overlord. I was not the one who should be hiding. She should be hiding from my fearsome vengeance.

In a rumbling purr that only we could hear, Obi-Squeekie-wan chastised the Annika and demanded that I and the Annoying One leave our hiding. Who did he think he was?

I lunged backwards out of the small space giving the Annika a face full of butt (which served her right). I raked my eyes over the room, looking for Squeekie – I had to remember that he might be Obi-Squeekie-wan to everyone else but he'd been Squeekie to me so many naps ago. Could he be my Squeekie again? No way. I was the Feline Overlord, not his underling.

"Kitties," said She of the Laps. "It's time to eat, and I don't want to see any more fighting."

A soft roar of excitement went up from us as we raced to the bowls for the kibble. I had to push the Annika away from my bowl.

"Eekak," Squeekie commented. I ignored him. He didn't have the right to chastise me for being more like a dog when it came to food, instead of a delicate flower who nibbled. Sexist that he was. I should bite him ... after dinner.

With a full belly, I was less interested in biting and found my usual spot on The Lap, having beaten the Annoying One who was sucking up to Squeekie. He'd learn soon enough that Squeekie was not any different than any other cat who'd figure out the Way of the Beloved Kitty. It just involved restraint and a little deceit, like pretending to like the brushes and the kisses. Although the kisses on top of my head weren't too bad.

The Annika sat on the rug staring up at me on The Lap. She was trying to intimidate me with her gaze. Hah! I was much savvier than that.

"Erp," said Squeekie as he jumped up and squeezed onto The Lap with me.

"Graw," I replied, reminding him that here he was just any other cat, not the Master of the Way of the Beloved Kitty. He purred a laugh.

"Betsi," said She of the Lap. "Be nice."

Squeekie just gave me a slit-eyed stare of triumph. I wiggled to take over more of The Lap, but he didn't budge. I was stuck if I wanted to stay on The Lap. I tried to find a more comfortable position, it brought me against Squeekie. He was warm and his purr rumbled like burbling water. I relaxed. It was nearly like old times, when we'd shared a bed at the Book Store. When we'd worked together on the Way of the Beloved Kitty. It was good.

"Annika," said She of the Lap. "jump up here with us?"

What? I lifted my head to glare. There was no more room on The Lap. The Annika was not welcome. She jumped up anyway squeezing into the space beside She of the Lap.

We are making the human happy, Squeekie purred.

Hah! Of course he would say that. He had the most lap, and he didn't have a mouthful of the Annika fur.

She doesn't belong here, I grumbled back to him.

His purr didn't change tones as he chastised me, *She is still learning. This is a test.*

I snorted. *Test. She's OLD. She should be put outside. She should be put in a cage if she hasn't learned by now.*

Then Squeekie did something he'd only done once as we'd been trained together, he growled. *Down. You must get down if you cannot follow The Way.*

No, I snapped back with a short "growl."

Now, Squeekie insisted with a paw on my neck. I reacted before I thought and bit his ear.

I was taken from The Lap before I had a chance to protest. The Annika slunk into my place, a triumphant curl to her tail as she snuggled against Squeekie.

After a night of hiding in the dark space by the crinkly paper where the Annoying One was not allowed, I came to the food bowl with a new attitude. I would ignore Squeekie and the Annika.

I looked through them, even when Squeekie purred and tried to butt me with his head. He thought he could make up now. He was so wrong.

I found a spot where the sun came through a window, heating the floor and warming my fur. The Annoying One always left me as I sunbathed. His fluff made him shun the sun. Not so Squeekie who sauntered over and sat in front of me.

"Yrr," I said, telling him he was blocking the heat.

I am? he purred back. *So sorry.* But he didn't move.

Stay or go? No way was I leaving. This was my home and my sun. I sat up, facing Squeekie. *Move*, I growled.

No, he purred.

When had he become more annoying than the Annoying One? Always. He'd always acted like he knew best, that he was the only one who knew exactly how to deal with humans. But we weren't learning anymore. I had gotten my title years ago and I didn't have to prove anything to him or the Annika. I swatted his head, a smack

My Distant Love

loud enough to catch his attention and unfortunately the attention of She of the Laps.

"Betsi," she said, lifting me from the floor and carrying me from the sun, from Squeekie who mewled *Who's got the sun now?*

Bowls and bowls of kibble later, Squeekie had taken over The Lap and was given the best spot for the sun. I'd had to put up with him, but tonight while She of the Laps slept, I was going to let Squeekie know that he wasn't welcome. Neither he nor the Annika.

I slinked down the steps and found Squeekie on *my* seat. I didn't make a noise. I jumped up silently. Squeekie was awake before my paw hit the soft and warm seat.

What do you want? he meowed.

I want you to stop taking my spot in the sun and The Lap.

He didn't answer immediately. *They aren't mine to give. It's not me who has stopped you.*

Liar, I said with a low growl, getting close enough that our noses touched. Instead of biting the soft underside of his neck, I bumped my forehead against his. That's not what I'd meant to do. We didn't move. Head bumps like this were only shared between cats who cared for each other. I certainly didn't care for or about Squeekie ... not anymore.

Why did you do that? he asked in a low purr. For once, he didn't sound calm and Zen. He sounded as shaken as I felt. I raced away and hid. What should I do? I didn't care for Squeekie. That was so long ago and he'd made it clear then that whatever I might have thought was between us didn't matter because his path to becoming a Master in the Way of the Beloved Kitty was more important. Now, that he was Obi-Squeekie-wan, he was a different cat. He wasn't the Squeekie that I'd ...yes, I'd fallen in love with.

I stayed in my hiding place through morning kibble and didn't venture out even when the door was opened to allow the sun on the rug that was *mine* — even the Annoying One understood that.

I didn't know what I was going to do with all of the feelings racing through me, so the best thing to do seemed to be to stay hidden.

"Merwr," Squeekie said, calling my name and telling me to come out of hiding.

I didn't respond, pretending I was asleep. He came closer. I caught that special Squeekie scent and heard his light purr (that went straight to my heart) as he went on speaking to me.

We had something special, Betsi, you know that, and last night, well, it was a reminder that there may have been things that we left unfinished. I know that I was so focused on the Way all those kibbles and naps ago, but ... well, I think, I ... we deserve another chance.

How had he gotten so close while he'd purred? He was less than an inch from my hiding place.

"Murp?" he asked if he could enter. How could I say no?

Squeekie squeezed in beside me and it was so familiar that I purred with joy, forgetting that I was mad at him, at the world, forgetting everything but how right it felt to be snuggled with Squeekie, fur to fur. We adjusted our bodies into the familiar position. Our heads rested on the other, so we could breathe in our scents. I sighed in contentment, and Squeekie breathed out a purr of bliss.

Long naps later, I heard her approach. She thought she was so stealthy, but the Annika was like an elephant in a bubble-wrap factory. Squeekie stirred too and gave a grumbling, "Mewrp," asking the Annika what she wanted.

"K-hiss," she responded making direct eye contact with me. If she wanted a fight, I would give her one. This was my house and this was *my* Squeekie!

I stood and puffed out my tail, making it nearly as fluffy as hers. My hiss was deeper and much more menacing. I stood in front of Squeekie even as he tried to nudge me out of the way.

"Yowl," I howled so that she and everyone else could hear. *Get out and stay out.*

She didn't flinch. She didn't crouch. She continued to stare. Swat, swat, her paw smacked me twice on the top of the head.

It was on. I leapt forward mouth open and fangs at the ready. Who was the Double Fanged Terror, now, I screeched at her, not even sure what I was saying.

Bald witch, howled the Annika.

We broke apart to circle and growl. I looked for an opening, a way to get to her throat. She was going down. On our third tight circle, Squeekie burst between us, "Meowawr," he said firmly and quietly, telling the two of us to stop. I didn't move but my tail twitched and my growl didn't lose its volume. As soon as he stepped away, I was going to surprise attack the Annika.

Squeekie turned to me. *You know better*, he mewled in low disappointment. *You are a Beloved Kitty. You could have made it in further, but you chose to come to this home. We are not staying—*

"Me-rowr," I answered pointing out that we had bumped heads and shared a bed.

"Gr-purr," he grumbled, explaining he'd been tired and remembering our days as young cats, not much more than kittens. What he'd done had been a mistake. He purred longer and lower with the soft painful words that he'd be returning to the Bookstore with the Annika. That he had more work with her and with the other cats who came to him for help. He could not be selfish and stay in a home.

"Grrowlll," I responded and shot off, low to the ground, as I raced to my super-secret spot ears flat. If the Annoying One came near, he'd get an earful. I didn't see him or even a human. My dark color blended in with the shadows of my space. I would just stay here until Squeekie and the Annika left. How dare he reject me like that and in front of another feline.

A nap later I was calmer and hungry, but I refused to leave my refuge. How much longer could they stay? I could out wait the human when she didn't want to let me on her lap, I could out wait His Jerkiness, Squeekie.

That was the plan until I realized that I could do without food and water, but not without THE BOX. Maybe I could wait until She of the Laps and the other felines went to sleep. That couldn't be too long. If I ran quickly, I could be there and out before Squeekie or The Annika knew.

"Ee-ack," I squeaked out naps and naps later when I slunk out of the hiding place and ran straight into Squeekie.

"Merp," he blurted out, telling me to stop because we needed to talk.

I didn't respond but raced to THE BOX, not worrying about stealth now and desperate. Maybe he'd be gone or I could find another hiding place?

No such luck. Squeekie stood and watched from a not-so-polite distance. When I had satisfactorily scraped the "dirt" in exactly the right way, I tried to walk past him, tail high. He stepped in front of me, blocking my way again.

"Mewp," he said as apology for bungling what he'd said.

I nearly fell over. Squeekie never apologized, even when in training he'd hit me so hard I'd fallen from above the book shelves to the floor.

"Gro-mew." OK. I hadn't meant to let him off the hook. What he'd done hadn't been OK. He'd led me on.

He moved closer and nuzzled at my ear with a purr, telling me I'd always been a great feline, that I could have gone far. "Merow," he said softly into my ear. He'd regretted many days that he'd chosen to stay at the Bookstore and teach the Way of the Beloved Kitty but it couldn't be changed now. We'd both chosen our paths. Even if he loved me, he couldn't stay.

My paw lashed out before I could stop it. *If* he loved me? He'd definitely loved me. He'd said it again and again. When it had come time to leave the Bookstore, he'd refused. I thought my heart would never heal. I was terrible to my human, forgetting the Way of the Beloved Kitty in my hurt. It had taken many naps and kibbles to get over the pain and remember my true purpose. And here was Squeekie again trying to ruin my life.

I didn't apologize for the smack, and Squeekie didn't follow me when I left.

I changed my routine to avoid Squeekie, eating after the others did, avoiding The Lap except when no other feline was nearby. I only saw him once and I quickly ran then, acting like I urgently need to be somewhere else.

Then, I heard She of the Laps on the phone and her words were better than tuna, Squeekie and The Annika would be leaving, that afternoon, which was three naps away. I raced around the house, excited by the noise, though I pretended that the old catnip mouse was the reason. Soon everything would be back to the way it should be. I would have The Laps. The Annoying One would be relegated to the edge. I would be the Feline Overlord, monarch of all I surveyed.

I found the perfect spot to watch the door for the arrival of the Cages of Travel. It only took part of one nap and there they were. They were more beautiful than my coat in the sun or a bird sitting on the ground within paw reach.

"Mer-urp?" asked the Annoying One, worried the cage might be for him. I happily explained that our visitors would be leaving. He was actually sad. Not even a nap later, Squeekie and the Annika were carried to the Cages. The humans stepped away and I went to the Squeekie cage. The Annika hissed. I ignored her.

"M-rowr," I said, telling Squeekie good riddance and don't come back.

He looked sad, his blue eyes swimming with unshed liquid. I would not weaken. We had been through years ago, why would I think a cat would change is lilac points. His soft "rorw" told me that he would miss me and that he'd never meant to hurt me. The Annika snorted.

He explained again softly but with such conviction that if I were able to step back from The Way of the Beloved Kitty, he would have, but his work was so important because he helped cats who'd been separated from humans and those who'd never known a human find places to stay for all the naps.

Plus, he added, *I've never failed to train at cat in the Way and The Annika is still not trained.*

That was the truth. That feline was a disgrace to the name. My heart still hurt, but I knew and had always known that Squeekie had a greater mission. I had to be content with the time we'd had together.

I bumped my head against the bars in apology and watched the Annika and Squeekie lifted away and back out of my life. The Annoying one cried pitifully, asking Obi-Squeekie-wan to stay because he still had so much to learn.

Faintly I heard Squeekie say, *Teach him, Betsi. You're a master now. You've sacrificed your happiness as I have for the betterment of all felines.*

I'd still much rather have Squeekie in my life than being a Master. I looked at the Annoying One and purred that I would continue to train him, but that he had to give up The Lap for 100 naps. He agreed and life went on, happily enough. I rarely thought of Squeekie over the next thousands of naps because I'd learned that the Way was something that could make my life better by helping others. Although sometimes late at night, I pretended that Squeekie was laying his head on me and giving me his special purrs.

My Distant Love

AUTHOR BIOGRAPHY

A former innkeeper and radio talk show host, **Heidi Hormel** has always been a writer. She spent years as a small-town newspaper reporter and as a PR flunky before settling happily into penning romances with a wink and a wiggle.

While living in the Snack Food Capital of the World, Heidi has trotted around the globe from forays into Death Valley to stops at Loch Ness in Scotland.

She has published five books in the Angel Crossing, Arizona series with Harlequin Western Romance. To sign up for her newsletter or to read more about her books, visit www.HeidiHormel.net or follow her on Facebook and Twitter.

Squeekie the Bookstore Cat

8

The Purrfect Tribute

Andrew Coons

Bzzz.

Squeekie, the renowned bookstore cat, twitched his ears without waking.

Bzzz.

His ears twitched again and he found himself dreaming of a rock concert. Instead of each cat playing a different instrument, however, all four were playing bass guitars. The hum created by the combined power of four bass guitars set his head to rattling. He restlessly tossed and turned on his perch by the window.

Bzzz.

Squeekie woke with a start. With a scornful meow he noted that the sound still persisted into the waking world.

What could possibly be making this reverberating cacophony at 2:30 in the morning?

He had thought that after he became accustomed to the sounds of the railyard, nothing short of the holy treat jar opening would be able to wake him. Yet here he was, in the middle of the night, shaking quite literally from the incessant low hum he felt more than heard.

What could possibly make such a powerful low pitched sound? It couldn't be a train, not even if it were four times as large as a normal train could it make such a racket! And if it was louder than a train, then that also ruled out any object inside the bookstore from being the source.

Squeekie reasoned that any vehicle or machine responsible for such an unearthly sound would have to be tremendously powerful.

He stood up slowly and stretched out his furry legs, body shaking from the reverberations, and gave out an obligatory yawn before plopping down onto the floor.

Squeekie padded towards the counter to check on his partner in crime Annika. Upon passing the clearing to the front door, he noticed a shimmering pale blue light streaking across the welcoming mat. Intrigued and convinced that Annika could handle herself in the interim, Squeekie changed course and headed straight towards the door without a lick of fear.

As he approached, the light sparkled across his face. He instinctively looked up and instantly had to look back down.

Ack, so blinding! Who would ever need so much light? he thought, rubbing a paw against his offended eyes.

He looked up again, this time with his paw blocking the worst of the light, but try as he might all he could see was the light itself. He sighed. He knew that he would have to use his secret door opening contraption he had installed after his diminutive height and lack of opposable thumbs made apparent the problem doors presented him.

Despite the late hour he cast a furtive glance around to make sure no one was looking, and then swept his paw under the bookcase adjacent to the door, felt, grasped, and then yanked on the secret lever hidden beneath. The door sprung open a good two feet and he pelted out before it sealed again.

Again, he looked *up* at the source of both the light and noise, wondering what on Earth it could be. Surely not a helicopter, it sounded nothing of the sort. Perhaps some sort of secret hi-tech hover jet?

Maybe, he thought, *but what on Earth would it be doing at the bookshop!? Surely the military has its own library!*

Squeekie noticed that the lights seemed to be pointed at an angle and there was a dark spot underneath their source where, just maybe, he would be able to solve this mystery. Caution long out the window, he bounded across the store's parking lot until he stood directly under the "thing".

He looked up but, try as he might, could not make out very much at all about what hovered above him, except that the casing holding the array of lights seemed to be circular. A moment later he noticed a small dot of the same pale blue light appear in the center of the dark spot that he swore hadn't been there not a moment before.

He squinted, his signature look, and his eyes quickly widened as he realized the dot was now a small ball, and growing larger by the second!

Before the thought that perhaps he should not be standing out in the opening even materialized in his head, a beam of light shot down directly towards him. He managed to let out a startled "Ack!" and then everything went pale blue.

A moment later and the store appeared as it always does at 2:34 A.M., the crickets chirped lazily, the store stood dark under the moonless sky, its thousands of transcribed stories resting safely within under lock and key. There was no blinding light, no incessant hum, not a single thing seeming out of place. That is, unbeknownst to anyone, with the exception of a small lonely red bow-tie laying forgotten and alone in the middle of the parking lot. The same red bow-tie Squeekie never takes off!

Squeekie's head pounded and his vision was blurry.

Ugh, what happened? He wondered.

A deep hum reverberated through his body and it all came back to him. The store! He wasn't at the store, but where else could he possibly be.

As his vision started to clear he was aware of a face-like shape resolving in front of his own. He blinked a few more times, looked at the face in front of him, and blinked a few more times.

Surely he wasn't staring face to face with a little Tasmanian penguin.

The penguin blinked back at him, curiosity evident in its eyes.

"I really need to see someone about these dreams I keep having" he said, hoping that was all it was, a dream.

He looked left and right and was greeted by an ocelot on the left, and on the right, a red panda. Their lifelike visage and the dull ache still residing in him didn't reassure him on this assessment. He noticed all three animals were behind bars.

Surely someone didn't kidnap him from the store just to take him to the zoo, he mused.

He snorted at the absurdity of...well, everything, and turned to find out more about where he was when he ran smack into another set of bars.

He let out an "oof" and couldn't help but whine a little.

How dare anybody lock up someone as magnificent as myself, he wondered disgruntledly.

Of course, he let his people at the bookstore lock him up from time to time so they could feel in charge. But he loved them, and they him, surely this wasn't there doing!

A tiny voice squeaked behind him - "Where are you going, friend?"

Squeekie turned around and faced the penguin whom he was sure had been the one speaking.

"Why, out of here, of course!" he said matter-of-factly. "That is, once I find a way out..."

"Good luck with that, the three of us haven't had the least bit of luck with it so far," she said glumly.

"I'm Pengu, by the way," she added, cheering up again.

"And you may have the honor of addressing me as Ossy" added the ocelot to Squeekie's left, inclining his head ever so slightly.

"And I'm Pan-Pan!" piped the red panda airily, sitting up on his haunches and grinning widely at Squeekie.

"The pleasure is mine," Squeekie said, bowing his head slightly to each of them in turn, "I am Squeekie the bookstore cat."

Although at the moment he hadn't the slightest idea where the bookstore was.

"So... where am I, I mean to say, where are *we* at exactly?" he asked.

The three looked at each other with a grin.

"You mean to say you haven't figured that out?" asked Ossy, with the barest tones of amusement. "Tell me, what is circular, flies in the sky, and abducts innocent cats and penguins, and yes, red pandas too" he added when Pan-Pan started to interrupt.

"Aliens! We're in a UFO!" Pan-Pan burst in, unable to help himself.

The Purrfect Tribute

He seemed a little too high-spirited for the situation, Squeekie noted.

"Quite right," Ossy added, "you don't mean to tell me you were taking a catnap when they got you?"

"Of course not," Squeekie said indignantly.

At that moment they all heard a whooshing noise and went quiet.

"Door opened, *they* are coming!" whispered Pengu.

They all stilled as something shuffled closer. Squeekie found himself suddenly anxious, expecting the aliens to look like some kind of savage otherworldly beast...like a dog.

He was surprised when it rounded the corner and he was face to face with a purple furred cat. Except for it was no cat at all, surely no type of cat has tentacles for ears! He let out a whine despite himself.

"%#*@&^. $)@*%&@!?" it blurted when it saw Squeekie.

It walked to a monitor across from Squeekie's cage and started tapping on the keyboard underneath. Squeekie quickly took stock of his surroundings. There was nothing in his cage besides the bars made out of metal and the roof made out of scratch board.

Wait, the roof made out of scratch board? he thought.

The alien "cat" started to turn around and Squeekie leapt into action, making up a plan as he went. Squeekie jumped straight up.

When the alien turned around it was surprised to see no Squeekie cat where there had been one not even a minute ago.

It made another garbled sound and walked to the cage door, pressing its paw print against a scanner. The door swung open and the alien stepped inside looking around warily.

Squeekie, holding onto the ceiling of his cage for dear life, tried to flatten himself out as much as possible. He waited until the alien walked directly beneath him and let go. He fell, letting out his signature squeak, and landed squarely on top of the alien, giving it quite a surprise.

He pounced off and ran out the door, quickly swinging it shut. He let out a sigh of relief when he heard the door close with a thud and the lock engage once again.

He couldn't help himself and swaggered back and forth in front of his new captive as his newfound friends cheered his heroics.

"Top notch," commented Ossy, quite impressed.

"That was amazing, Squeekie! I wish I could fly as high as you just did!" Pengu said looking up at her own cage's ceiling.

"I wanna be just like you, Squeekie!!" cheered on Pan-Pan, bursting with enthusiasm, already pouncing back and forth on all fours, reenacting Squeekie's daring escape.

Looking very smug, Squeekie basked in their praise. Though he knew now was not the time to sit around too long.

"Listen, tell me where to find their leader and I'll put an end to 'em all!"

Pengu, the captive held longest, told Squeekie all that she knew.

He stretched out his front legs once and then he was off, with his three friends calling out encouragements after him.

He started off the way the alien had come in, bounding out through what passed as doors here and headed down the adjoining corridor. He went left at this intersection, then right at the next, and so on, careful to keep an eye out for more aliens.

He had one close call when he heard muffled footsteps approaching the same intersection as him. He looked around desperately for somewhere to hide and had to settle with flattening himself inside a tiny alcove in the wall, glad his dull grey coat matched the surrounding material.

He risked a glance towards the intersection and saw a patrol of the aliens marching in step, their tentacle ears bouncing in unison. One of the alien cats began to turn its head towards him until its partner marching beside it let out what sounded like a conversational "%@#$@^*)..?". The alien cat looked backed towards its partner and the procession carried on out of sight.

Squeekie blew out a long breath he hadn't realized he was holding and proceeded on his way. The rest of his short journey on the ship passed without incident, however he did peek in a few open doors along the way to discover even more of his fellow earth

The Purrfect Tribute

animals jailed within. He swore he even heard a whale's sing song voice emanating from one room.

A whale! On a spaceship! How preposterous!

He finally found what appeared to be the bridge of the spaceship, his target, and without hesitating dashed headlong into the center of the room...a room filled with countless alien cats.

He looked left and right and hissed loudly, daring them to look him in the eye. As he looked around they all lowered their eyes. One alien cat, whom he assumed was the captain held his gaze longer than the rest, but still ultimately had to look away. He decided to address her.

"You! Captain of this ship!" he wasn't sure if she really was the captain or if she even understood what he was saying. "Listen to me now, you!"

Every alien cat was transfixed on Squeekie as he stomped his front paws up and down as he yelled out to them.

"This is no way to treat other animals! You can't just take us from our homes and do whatever weird alien experiments you wish on us! No!" he said, adding in a hiss here and there for effect.

"We have families and lives too! We're not your guinea pigs! Guinea pigs aren't your guinea pigs either!" he added, not wanting any future guinea pig abductions on his paws.

"Now here is what you will do! Are you listening!?" he stomped his feet some more, as much to intimidate them as to vent his own frustration. "You will take us back to our homes immediately! No delays! You will put each and every one of us back where you found us, exactly as you found us, and you won't take any more captives without their consent!"

"Don't you even know how traumatic this whole episode has been for us all?" Squeekie went on, feeling that he was on a roll. "I could eat as many treats as I want for the rest of my life and that still wouldn't assuage the nightmares I'll have! Think before you just go cat snatching whatever poor bookstore cat you just happen to pass by!"

"Now what are you waiting for!? Take us back right this instance!"

He stomped his feet one last time and then again looked around the room at each alien cat. Every alien cat again lowered his or her gaze, except for this time the cat he had pegged as the captain held his gaze and after a short pause, nodded and then bowed slightly. The other alien cats mimicked their captain and amid the bowing alien cats, Squeekie felt a triumphant grin breaking across his face.

Within the hour the spaceship hovered over a thick forest somewhere in China.

Squeekie looked out a floor window and watched as Pan-Pan hovered down the same beam that had captured him at the bookstore. Pan-Pan made a spectacle of it, doing flips and somersaults in midair. When he landed he did his Squeekie imitation hopping into the air and then settled down onto his haunches, grinning madly, and waved up at the ship as it receded out of view.

Within moments they were over a small beach filled with penguins in Tasmania. Pengu dived into the water at the end of her beam-ride and surfaced, waving a wing at the ship as it once again continued on its journey.

Quite a few stops later and half a world away they reached the thick jungles of Central America. Ossy endured his beam-ride with perfect dignity, landing lightly on his padded feet. He turned and looked up at the ship and nodded once, before turning and bounding into the brush.

Shortly after they finally arrived back in Enola, Pennsylvania, hovering over top Squeekie's bookstore. It felt like he had been away for several days, although in actuality it had only been the previous night that he had been abducted.

As he made his way to the beaming pad, the alien captain and most of the crew came to see him off. They bowed again, as if to say sorry. He nodded and suddenly found himself floating down towards a now full bookstore parking lot.

He landed lightly on his feet, right on top of his bowtie. After managing to get the bowtie on again, in the mysterious and unknown way in which cats manage to do things normally requiring opposable thumbs (like opening doors), he waited for a customer to walk into the bookstore and snuck in behind her. He marveled that no one appeared to have noticed the flying saucer hovering above the bookstore.

"I don't know where he has gotten off to today, I haven't seen him at all," he heard one of his humans saying to one of the customers. "I always wonder what he's up to when he goes missing for part of the day, probably on some grand adventure," his human said laughing, as if it were some sort of joke.

Ah well, he thought to himself, *better play the part that is expected of me*.

He faked a long kitty yawn and hopped up onto the counter between his human and the customer and resumed his role as bookstore cat.

Later that night after the store had closed and the humans left, Squeekie was in front of the computer screen watching the nightly news.

"And now for the weirdest story of the year, one unlike anything that our viewers will have ever heard of or seen before. Across the globe food, yes food, has been raining from the sky from some unknown source," the anchor stated, a little wide-eyed herself.

"There have been reports of herrings raining in Tasmania, meat fillets in the jungles of Guatemala, savory bamboo shoots in the jungles of China, and our latest report has indicated cat treats, yes cat treats, have been falling in a small town in Pennsylvania!" the news reporter stated with bafflement to a now empty desk, as Squeekie had already bounded to the front door.

He looked outside and sure enough the entire parking lot was filled with cat treats, enough to last him, Annika, and all his cat buddies a lifetime...or ten! His eyes were as large as tennis balls as he watched in wonderment as more and more treats rained down.

He suddenly recalled his words to the alien cat captain... 'I could eat as many treats as I want for the rest of my life and that still wouldn't assuage the nightmares I'll have!'

Squeekie grinned the smuggest grin a cat could ever grin as he reached for his secret door opening contraption.

Well, he thought as he walked out the door, *I was never going to have any nightmares, but no one needs to know that now!*

The Purrfect Tribute

AUTHOR BIOGRAPHY

Andrew Coons is a computer aficionado who loves reading old fashioned print books. He works with Squeekie the Bookstore at the bookstore by day, and enjoys adventuring through video games and the pages of books by night.

Squeekie the Bookstore Cat

Squeekie Celebrates 20 Years of Cupboard Maker Books

Note on Stories 9 - 20

Stories 9 through 20 were chosen by bookstore customers voting on their favorite Squeekie stories from *The First Nine Lives of Squeekie the Bookstore Cat* and *The Second Nine Lives of Squeekie the Bookstore Cat*. They are presented in order of most votes and are the same stories that appear in the first two Squeekie books, with only small editorial changes.

If you read the first two Squeekie books, we thank you from the bottom of our hearts for supporting the store, and hope you enjoy re-reading these stories again.

Squeekie the Bookstore Cat

9

Way of the Beloved Kitty

Heidi Hormel

I am the Double Fanged Terror, slayer of stinkbugs and killer of Mousey-Mouse. I rule my domain with razor teeth and Claws of Steel. Watch me fly through the air like a dragon ninja.

I will amuse myself with my musings and my acrobatics.

"Cat," My Human says as I test my claws on the Cat Who Gets All the Laps. She will know that this reclining throne is mine. *Scratch, scratch.* "Stop it," says My Human again. I glance with disdain, shaking my fluffy brown and cream fur into order. I am the Double Fanged Terror.

Then the liquid of death hits my shoulder. I must run from the water, the bringer of feline humiliation. I find a safe space under the fortress of human food and lick my water wounds. It tastes better than it feels.

I peer from beneath the fortress's veil, watching for My Human and the She Who Gets All the Laps. I will nap to reserve my strength.

"Richard," My Human says, but I keep my eyes closed. If I cannot see her, she cannot see me. "Ricky." She's getting closer. Then hands around me. I struggle for a moment.

These meetings often end in Delightful Treats. I calm myself and watch over her shoulder. It's like being on top of the humming food box. I can watch everything around me. There is Mousey-Mouse. I must remember to come back and destroy him with my Blue Glare of Annihilation, even though he lacks the squeaks I love to hear as I vanquish my foes.

"Here he is," My Human says. "I know all of his hiding places."

"Mew, mew, mew," I yell my voice hoarse with embarrassing fear. It is MAL-OR-EE. The most terrifying Human in my domain.

I dig in my claws so I can leap to safety. My Human screams. The MAL-OR-EE makes a grab. I show my double fang — *No.* She touches me and I strike out with my front claw and I'm free. I race up the stairway to safety. I find the space that My Human and She Who Gets All the Laps don't fit.

Must slow my breathing. I got away. I am safe. I am the Double Fanged Terror. I do not ever need to be the Beloved Kitty, like She Who Gets All the Laps.

"Mew. Mew," I say. *Wait. What?* I'm picked up disturbing my Sleep of Restoration and put into the Box of Torture. It moves. I put out my Claws of Steel to keep from falling, then the noise of a machine and the sway. I hate the sway. It always ends in the Place of Bad Smells, where they poke me in places no cat should ever be poked. But the sway is different. It is longer. *Where are we going?* "Roar?" I try to get My Human's attention. She must stop. "Grr," I say for the first time ever. She must understand I am serious about the stopping. But she doesn't listen.

So long later that I cannot count the number of naps it would take, the swaying stops. I am still in the Box of Torture, but now we are outside, then we are in a new house that is not a house. I smell and hear other felines. It is not She Who Gets All of the Laps. Another one who smells — "Meowar."

The sound is familiar. Is it a new enemy? Or ... I bow down as he approaches the Box of Torture. It is the legend — Obi-Squeekie-wan. I lived with him many bowls of Crunchy Delights ago. Why have I been brought here again?

"I'm hoping you can help me with Richard. He runs from visitors and poor Mallory can't get near him," says My Human

Was the MAL-OR-EE here? Must hide. There is no place in the Box of Torture. I move, it sways.

"Stop that," says My Human. Finally the box is on solid ground.

"I'm not sure how we can help?" says another Human.

"Actually, I thought maybe Squeekie could show him how to get along with people? You know, like Richard could be his intern or something? Squeekie is a Siamese, too, even though he doesn't have long hair like Ricky, and he is so good with everybody including little kids."

"I don't know. We've haven't done anything like that before. What do you think, Squeekie?"

Way of the Beloved Kitty

"Maowar," answers Obi-Squeekie-wan. He is not pleased. He says that I cannot learn anything.

"Mew," I answer because I can learn. I am the Double Fanged Terror.

"Rrr." Obi-Squeekie-wan laughs at me.

My Human says, "I'm desperate. If he doesn't act better around Mallory, I may have to find him a new place. We've tried everything. Maybe he's just not happy at my house?"

What is My Human saying? That she'll leave me here? "Mew?" I ask. She doesn't answer, but Obi-Squeekie-wan does with a bump against the Box of Torture.

"Mewl?" he asks. *Are you ready to learn now? I tried to instruct you many Crunchy Delights ago, but you would not listen.*

"Mow." *I am ready and willing. I do not want to leave My Human.*

"OK," says the other Human.

"Great. I've brought food and his special toys." My Human's voice gets closer. "Ricky, I don't want to leave you here but you must learn. I'll bring you home as soon as I can because I know Mallory already misses you."

I look through the slots. *Is the MAL-OR-EE here?*

Obi-Squeekie-wan makes a low sound and bumps the Box of Torture again. He says that *the MAL-OR-EE is another Human, and I must learn that the short humans are even more important than the tall ones.*

*No way. They do not bring the Crunchy Delights and they **grab**.*

Here is your first lesson, Richard: Stop and they will not grab.

Before I can answer, the door on the Box of Torture is opened, and I am out like the wind of the night, past Obi-Squeekie-wan and off to find a Cave of Security.

"Ricky," My Human calls, but I must ignore her. No matter what Obi-Squeekie-wan says I cannot stay if the MAL-OR-EE is near.

I am hungry but there is the smell of other felines and Obi-Squeekie-wan says I may not have any Crunchy Delights until I can say hello to each one. I creep along the floor. I know she is near. Obi-Squeekie-wan says her name is Annika. She is like me, fluffy haired and puffy tailed, but her nose is short, not noble like mine. I see her. She stares at me. I look away as I've been taught by Obi-Squeekie-wan. Annika makes a low growl like She Who Gets All the Laps. I go lower to the floor so she cannot see me. Then Obi-Squeekie-wan says, *You must approach her or you will never become a Beloved Kitty.*

You can show me the way of the Beloved Kitty?

Of course, he answers, his light blue eyes sparkling.

I look up and to the side. Annika sits and watches me. I am brave. I am the Double Fanged Terror. I race to her. She swats me with a paw and it rings through my brain.

"Meow," says Obi-Squeekie-wan, telling me that I have approached Annika in every way that is wrong. In a low purr, he explains that I must approach her with respect.

"Mew," I say. *I am the Double Fanged Terror and she should respect me first.*

Obi-Squeekie-wan tells me he doesn't care. *If I want to be a Beloved Kitty that means respecting other felines and making friends, not enemies or minions.*

"Me-rowr," Obi-Squeekie-wan says. He and I will need to spend much time together at the Home of Books and Shelves until I understand exactly how to be a cat, the first step in becoming a Beloved Kitty.

So begins my training in humiliation and respect. I must sleep with the kittens, even though I am a superior full-grown fluffy cat. I growl and swat the kittens who try to touch my tail. Obi-Squeekie-wan and Annika quickly come and discipline me.

I eventually learn to play without biting or taunting. Next, I learn to visit with Annika and she teaches me to groom fluffy fur properly and to stare without staring at the other felines.

When Obi-Squeekie-wan says that I am now past the first step in the Way of the Beloved Kitty. I purr with joy.

Many meals of Crunchy Delights later, I have passed the Stillness of Clipping, when the human takes silver to my nails. Then the pleasure-pain of the brush is endured. I could be one step closer to Beloved Kitty after today, Obi-Squeekie-wan says. It will be my greatest challenge so far. *The Human Carry, Pet, and Grab must be accepted and enjoyed.*

"Raowr," Obi-Squeekie-wan says, *Today there will be more humans than I have ever seen at the Home of Books and Shelves. My job will be to allow humans – no matter their size -- to touch me without running away.*

Way of the Beloved Kitty

The other felines look down on me from the Cloud Walks. Annika lays on the counter and sniffs as she says I am like her and will never be a Beloved Kitty. It is the curse of the Fluffy Cat. *We turn into wild animals at the touch of new humans.* Obi-Squeekie-wan tells her that she is wrong. He says Annika is not wild but a Scaredy Cat.

We all wait for the fight. Annika sniffs again and saunters away with a disdainful wave of her tail.

I watch Annika's fluffy tail and imagine the hands of strange humans touching and grasping me. Maybe I am a Cursed Fluffy Cat. My whiskers twitch. I do not want to do this, but I do want to be a Beloved Kitty.

I walk to Obi-Squeekie-wan and ask if there isn't another test. *I can jump from the highest Cloud Walk to the counter.* He says that it must be the strange humans. He stares at me and doesn't let me look away.

"Meow," he says because my stare shows bravery, certainly enough to face the strange humans. When I become a Beloved Kitty, Obi-Squeekie-wan says I will get extra Delightful Treats and the best thing ever, which I will only know after I become a Beloved Kitty. Do I want to miss that?

No. I am the Double Fanged Terror. I fear nothing, not even Strange Humans and their grasping hands.

I follow Obi-Squeekie-wan to the counter. There is a group of Small Humans. The worst kind. The kind that must be avoided.

"Mewl," says Obi-Squeekie-wan pushing me forward to my next test in the Way of the Beloved Kitty. *Stand up tall,* he tells me.

I try so hard to walk tall, not crouch so the small humans don't see me. I hear a jeer from Annika who reminds me I am a Cursed Fluffy Cat. But that's not what I want. I want to be a Beloved Kitty. I force my legs to un-crouch. Obi-Squeekie-wan points out to my ears. They are flat to my head. *That is not the proper position.*

"Look, Mommy," says a Small Human. "Fuffy kitty."

Steady, purrs my mentor. *Watch me.*

I stand in horror as I see Obi-Squeekie-wan go right up to the Small Human and get patted on the head then pulled into a squeezing hug. This is worse than anything I've ever seen. Ever. How can my mentor expect me to do that? How does he do that?

"Preddy kitty," says the Small Human and releases my mentor, who walks to another human for a pet and ... a Delightful Treat.

A Delightful Treat? That may be worth a grab by the Small Human. I move forward. The Small Human squeals. My ears lay down and Obi-Squeekie-wan growls so no one else hears except me and Annika. She sneers and purrs a chuckle.

I will be a Beloved Kitty. I am not afraid like Annika.

"Look, Mommy, another kitty" says the Small Human loud enough to break my ears. Obi-Squeekie-wan is watching.

I move closer and closer to the Small Human watching the hands with the graspy fingers. *I can do this. I am the Double Fanged Terror.*

"Meow," says Obi-Squeekie-wan, reminding me I must go closer or I will never be a Beloved Kitty.

I slip one paw nearer. I allow my tail to go straight up and put my ears into the happy pose. The Small Human squeals again. My ears don't move. I place my paw closer, Claws of Steel sheathed.

The Small Human lunges forward, hand out and her fingers pat hard on my head. My eyes close, but I don't move.

"Careful, honey," says a Large Human.

"Maowr," says Obi-Squeekie-wan. *Don't move. Don't scratch. Don't growl.*

I nearly lose my nerve when the face of the Small Human comes closer, followed by a smooch on the top of my head.

"Grr," says Annika and races away. She is disappointed I have not failed this hardest test.

The Small Human gives me one more pat and moves away.

"Blurp," I say. *I have passed the test.*

Obi-Squeekie-wan says, *You have more tests, but you have done well.*

I strut through the Home of Books and Shelves. I allow one more human to touch me without running and without moving my ears. This is easy.

Today is the final, final test. If I pass it, I will become a Beloved Kitty (and get special Crunchy Delights). I walk around the Home of Books and Shelves, my tail waving and my ears in happy pose. The other felines on their way to Beloved Kitty look at me in awe.

Annika flattens her ears and laughs at me. "K-hiss," she says. *Fluffy Cats are cursed.*

I'm ready to bump her nose when Obi-Squeekie-wan calls me. *It is time.*

Way of the Beloved Kitty

I saunter to the front of the store to stand with Obi-Squeekie-wan. He reminds me, *You cannot run away. You cannot growl. You cannot scratch. And, most importantly, you cannot bite.*

"Meowr," I say with confidence. *I've got this. I have passed all the other tests. I will pass this one. I am the Double Fanged Terror.*

"Mew," says Obi-Squeekie-wan. *Don't be so sure. This is not like the others.*

My mentor stares at me. I have learned to look down and not challenge him.

"Blerp?" I ask, wondering when the test will start. Obi-Squeekie-wan eyes glance to the door. My test is here.

I sit as Obi-Squeekie-wan does, my eyes closed enough to look like I'm snoozing, calm with my ears in sleepy pose. I wait.

"Richard," My Human says. My eyes pop open.

"Mew," Obi-Squeekie-wan says quietly. *This is not the test.*

Still, I stand and put my tail in the air and ears in happy pose. My Human gives me pets and pats. They all feel good, not like they used to.

"Ricky," the MAL-OR-EE says.

I freeze. A protest growls through me.

"Maowr," says Obi-Squeekie-wan. *No growling.*

But this is the MAL-OR-EE. He does not understand. I must get away. I cannot—

"Richard, we're here to take you home. You're ready now," My Human says as she and the MAL-OR-EE swarm around me.

I can't breathe. I must get away. I climb the MAL-OR-EE with my claws of steel. Must get to the Cloud Walks. I leap. I yowl louder than the MAL-OR-EE.

Annika chuckles.

I pant on the walkway. Obi-Squeekie-wan shakes his head in disgust. My Human glares at me. The MAL-OR-EE cries.

I run low to the walkway and find a dark corner to hide. My breathing slows. How did I ever think I could become a Beloved Kitty. Annika was right. I am a Cursed Fluffy Cat.

I hear the other felines munching on Delightful Treats. I am not hungry. I cannot show my disgraced self.

"Richard," says My Human. "Come here kitty. Come on kitty." There is a long pause. I can only hear the crunching. "Maybe we'll have to leave him here if he isn't any better with Mallory."

Leave me. No. But I have failed. I am not a Beloved Kitty. I crouch further into my dark hole.

"He doesn't mean it," says the MAL-OR-EE. "Maybe Squeekie just needs more time to teach him manners. Please. Can't we wait. I love him so much."

Love me? The MAL-OR-EE loves me? I never imagined that. She always grabbed me, chased me. What had Obi-Squeekie-wan said? *Stop. Wait. And, then, no grab. You teach them by not moving.* Was that true? Yes. It had worked with the even smaller humans.

I creep from my dark hole. "Blu-urp," I say. *Wait.* I race along the Cloud Walk. "Blu-urp."

"Meoawr," says Obi-Squeekie-wan. *Hurry.*

I scamper along the planks and leap to the floor, running faster and faster. There they are. By the clear doors. "Mewl," I say. *Don't leave.* The MAL-OR-EE turns. I hesitate. She will grab me and then— She'll love me. That's why she grabs me.

"Mew," says Obi-Squeekie-wan. *Now, you understand.*

I stop in front of the MAL-OR-EE. "Mewlor," I say. *Don't leave without me.*

"Ricky," she says. Her grasping hands reach out. I do not move. I am as still and calm as Obi-Squeekie-wan. Her hand does not grab. It pets. My Human stands behind her now, smiling at me.

"Oh, what a good boy," she says. "He likes you."

I wouldn't go that far, but—

"Maowr," says Obi-Squeekie-wan, reminding me that I am nearly a beloved kitty. I must not move. I must accept the pats, pets, hugs, and kisses from the MAL-OR-EE. My ultimate test.

"Ricky," the MAL-OR-EE says and grasps me in a big hug.

I do not move, then the squeeze feels good on my sides. I bump my head against her chin to let her know that I understand she loves me and I love her.

"Mewlr," says Obi-Squeekie-wan. *You are a Beloved Kitty.* The other felines cheer. Annika sniffs with disdain.

As I leave, held in the arms of the MAL-OR-EE, I say, "Mewl," to Annika. *One day you will be brave enough to be a Beloved Kitty.*

"Grrrl," she answers. *Never.*

"Blerp," I say just before the doors close. *You can teach an old cat new tricks.*

Way of the Beloved Kitty

AUTHOR BIOGRAPHY

A former innkeeper and radio talk show host, **Heidi Hormel** has always been a writer. She spent years as a small-town newspaper reporter and as a PR flunky before settling happily into penning romances with a wink and a wiggle.

While living in the Snack Food Capital of the World, Heidi has trotted around the globe from forays into Death Valley to stops at Loch Ness in Scotland.

She has published five books in the Angel Crossing, Arizona series with Harlequin Western Romance. To sign up for her newsletter or to read more about her books, visit www.HeidiHormel.net or follow her on Facebook and Twitter.

Squeekie the Bookstore Cat

10

Hide and Go Squeek

Eric Hardenbrook

"Hey mister, why are you out here?" The young man strolled up to the ramshackle table set up beside the door.

"Yeah," added the girl walking with him, "Why aren't you in there, where the rest of the books are?"

The man shifted and his folding, portable chair squealed in protest. "I am out here because I get to see all the customers before they even get inside. How much better can you get?"

"Sure, I guess. But it's hot out here in this weather, or humid. I forget," the girl squinted and looked up.

"Yeah, and it looks like it might rain," added the boy.

"Well, I have my portable shelter with me as well," the man gestured up. His shelter looked vaguely like four umbrellas that had been poorly stitched together.

"I guess," the boy didn't sound convinced.

"Well, I'm not here to talk about the weather or shelter arrangements, I'm here to sell my newest book!" the man waved his arm in grandiose fashion across the stack of slender volumes arranged in front of him. "I'm the author of these fine," and just as he was about to launch into his sales pitch the door swung open between him and his potential customers stopping his conversation.

Jay, the other author present for the signing event was holding the handle of the door while chatting with a couple just leaving, "Thanks so much for dropping by folks. Thanks again, I'm sure you'll enjoy all three of my new books. Be sure to stop back and tell Michelle what you think of them." Then he turned and went back into the store pulling the door closed behind him.

"Hey mister, who was that?" the girl asked.

"That was Mr. Smith. He is the other author here for the signing today. Now as I was saying…"

"Yeah, but he's inside," the boy followed on the girl's thoughts.

"Yes. Yes, he is. So is that stupid cat."

"OH! We love the cats!" the girl gushed. She missed the attitude that radiated from the man sitting there.

"Yeah, totally. They're so cool that they climb and get to go wherever they want," the boy looked envious.

"What particular cat do you mean?" The girl asked.

"Squeekie of course. It's the only one that's always here! But I don't want to talk about that, I want you to see the book," and the door opened again to stop the conversation. Smith shaking hands and waving folks off with another copy of his book.

"Squeekie is our favorite!" The boy started again as soon as the door closed.

"Yeah, he's so cute I just want to hug him," the girl hugged herself and twisted back and forth for emphasis.

"He is not cute. He's constantly trying to climb all over me. It doesn't matter when I come in or where I try to set up." The author slumped back into his portable chair. "The very first time I came in for a signing he clawed a hole in my pant leg trying to get in my lap."

"Well, just pick him up. Duh." The boy seemed less than impressed with a single hole in a pair of pants.

"I will not. I don't like cats."

"How do you write books if you don't like cats?" The girl raised a single eyebrow in question. "I thought that was like a requirement or something."

"NO, it most certainly is not." The author leaned forward, warming to this new subject. "Cats and all other manner of pets are a nuisance. They distract from the actual writing."

"No, they don't. Ms. Michelle has a whole book of stories about her cat." The boy waved at the poster on the door. "And she keeps a bunch of other ones until they find their forever homes."

"Yes, that's all well and good for her, but I don't like them. I didn't much like the hole in my pants, but I could let that go. The second time I came in I set up in front of the door where Mr. Smith is now. No sooner was the table level then the cat's up there getting in the way and knocking over my soda."

"Oh, you know he didn't mean that, he probably just wanted to help." The girl glanced wistfully at the door. "I really like playing with the cats when I'm here. Sometimes I don't even look at the books," the girl looked ashamed, as if it were some kind of crime.

"That's my point..." and the door swung open between them again. A group of three older children were walking out all holding a copy of Smith's latest book.

"Look, will you two please move a little closer to me over here?"

"Sure, but you wouldn't have this problem if you were inside," the boy didn't seem to notice the glare that comment earned him from the author.

"I was inside for that signing. I couldn't keep anything standing upright on the table. That cat kept knocking everything over. IF he wasn't knocking things over he was yowling and laying down on top of everything."

"Cat's don't yowl, they meow." The girl smiled while she closed her eyes doing her best impression of gloating when one knows the answer and others don't.

"That one yowls. So I moved my table for the next signing. I went to the table back by the bathroom. That wasn't any better - the cat was back there constantly." The author's consternation at reliving the whole scenario was beginning to turn into a sour mood.

"Well, couldn't somebody pick the cat up for you?" They both seemed to think that was an excellent solution.

"Yes, we tried that. The next time I was in I called ahead. I asked them to give me a spot near the shelves holding the staff picks. I thought that would be a much better solution. As it turned out the cat simply leapt down from one of those boards that run all over the place and tried to land on the diagonal shelf. That didn't work entirely as the cat planned so he caromed off that and onto me again."

Both the boy and the girl giggled. "I bet that was funny," the girl added.

"Hardly." The author crossed his arms.

"Well, that still doesn't explain why you're out here," the boy said.

"I tried a table by the door. I tried a table in the back. I tried a table by the shelves up front. No place I went seemed to work." The author leaned forward and put an arm on either side of the table. "So the next time I came into the store I sent a text ahead again. I asked Michelle to let me use a spot in the expansion area toward the back of the store. She was happy to oblige, but no sooner did I set up my little corner back there then that darn cat pokes its head out of the shelf right next to me and tries to climb onto my shoulder! I even brought my own daughter to the store so she could occupy the cat. Squeekie wanted nothing to do with her – wouldn't go near her."

"Wow, he really likes you." the girl sounded so sincere the author couldn't shout his reply at her.

"Yes, but as I stated before I don't like him."

"You should, it would be easier." The boy seemed determined.

"It would not. In fact I took part in another signing day when the tables were all downstairs in the basement and within 5 minutes that cat had tracked me down there and was knocking things off my table!" The author was red faced and sweating. The humid weather was starting to get to him.

"Oh, we don't like the basement it's super creepy," the girl shuddered.

"I like it even if you don't," the boy puffed his chest out. "I went down there during one event and they turned the lights out on us for a whole five minutes" he went on proudly.

"Yes, it's a wonderful and creepy space but still plagued by cats. Now however I have won our little game of hide and seek. I am here and he can't get out to torment me. Listen, I'd like to tell you about the books I've got here," and once again just as the author attempted to describe his work the door swung open.

"There you two are. Would you please come inside?" A kind looking lady waved her arm at the children, "Come on! We don't have a ton of time today, and besides, it's starting to rain. Let's go!" She smiled and both of the children turned and trotted into the store.

"Good luck mister," the girl waved and pulled her arm back in just as the door swung shut.

The author blew out the breath he didn't realize he'd been holding. How could one miserable cat be such a ridiculous bother? He glanced up as the patter of raindrops began on his shelter. He heaved another deep breath and shifted his table a little further back from the edge of his shelter.

Just as he thought he might be safe and the rain just a passing shower a stiff breeze swept across the parking lot and the rain began in earnest. He glanced up at his shelter while he warily slid some plastic over the top of his books. So long as the wind didn't get out of control he'd be just fine.

Hide and Go Squeek

As soon as the thought crossed his mind the door swung open and the mother of the two children he'd been chatting with came back out. Her back was to him as she backed up against the door handle and pushed her umbrella out and open. "Come on you two, I told you we didn't have much time," she was waving the two children back out to the parking lot. The boy dodged out to the leading edge of the umbrella immediately sticking one hand out into the rain. The girl was close behind and turned her head to look back into the store. The author stood reaching a hand out toward the door. That's when the author saw the cat. It was Squeekie and he was making a dash for the door.

Just like a movie, the actions of everyone slowed down in the author's mind. The little girl turned and bent to stop the cat from escaping the store. Her mother spun awkwardly in an attempt to both keep her son reasonably dry and out of the rain while reaching back for her daughter. She backed up a half step pushing the door past normal extension. The door knocked into the front leg of the makeshift shelter.

Just as the author shifted and looked up to judge the possible damage the sagging patch in the center of his little roof gave way and dumped the puddle of rainwater directly onto his head. The chilly water made him roar in frustration. He slapped his hands down on the plastic covering his books to save them and turned his now dripping head back toward the door.

In the moment he glanced back he saw the cat stop. Just stop and sit down on the floor. The family bustled out to their car completely oblivious to the author's plight. The author sighed and ran his hands back over the top of his head to push some of the water back up out of his face. At that moment the cat stood up, turned and walked away from the door as if to say, "my work here is done".

"Fine," the author grumbled as he stuffed books back into boxes. "You win this time cat, but I'll be back and next time I'll figure out a place to sign where you won't be able to get at me."

Eric Hardenbrook

AUTHOR BIOGRAPHY

Eric is a fan, an author and an artist, usually in that order. Eric lives in central Pennsylvania with his gorgeous wife and daughter. He writes to try to get the stories out of his head. When he's being a fan he helps run Watch the Skies and assists in the publication of their monthly fanzine. He can be found (at least some of the time) at The Pretend Blog. When not working on those things, Eric enjoys the occasional video or board game and is an old school role player.

11

Squeekie vs. the Stinkie Apocalypse

Jay Smith

This dude at the front door didn't sit right with me.

I mean, I live – *lived* – in a book store where all sorts of folks dropped by. I'm not one to judge because people are people and so long as they don't mess with me or my foster brothers and sisters, I'm happy to see them. I like scritches and treats and the occasional, gentle belly rub and I don't care who's offering.

But this dude: he was not right.

Let me back up.

I live – (sigh) *lived* – in a big cinderblock warehouse. Far as I understood the arrangement, I owned the place. Michelle and Jason ran a book store out of it so they could keep me fed and happy. They did a really good job, too. A lot of people came in all the time to buy books. Sometimes they might scoop a bunch of books into their arms and buy them all. I don't get it, but the books make people happy and selling those books keeps me happy because – food, scratches, toys, and fun.

Well, until lately, that is. But I'll get to that.

Don't give me that. I'm a cat. I'll get to it when I'm ready. *Chill, brah.*

I asked my foster brothers and sisters if their homes are like this and most of them look at me funny. They came from much different places than this or even the streets. When they arrive, they're usually a little nervous or sad but I did my best to share my world with them and get them to relax. I tell them not to mind the grumpy cat – *Annika* – behind the counter but give her a wide berth because, well, she's moody. Most of the fosters call her worse, but I think even Annika has a good heart. She's just...well, a *cat*.

Jay Smith

The fosters are cats who stop over here on their way to a forever home. Some of them are a little weird from being alone or abused but I try my best to make them welcome and feel safe. Some are just kittens who don't know anything but the inside of a cage. Others spent their lives on the streets and have a real hard time trusting anybody and, so, spend the most time here waiting for that right person or people to come along.

Right now, my family, aside from Annika, is made up of two kittens, a "chocolate swirl" tabby called *Irving* and his "peanut butter swirl" sister, *Petunia*. They are a bundle of energy and so cute together. We also have *Captain Fabulous*; a mature and laid back Scottish Fold with curly ears and a wrinkled face who was surrendered to a shelter when his hippie owners entered what he called "old people forever camp." Cap Fab is a lot of fun, but likes "the nip" probably a little too much.

Usually, at night, everybody leaves and I get to be alone with my thoughts. I was considering writing an opera or maybe get all of us together to stage a musical version of my first Nine Lives for people. I needed something awesome to follow up my super-awesome bestselling book but I didn't want the same-old same-old.

But one night, Michelle, her family, and a few other folks turned up around the time the moon was high in the sky. They shut off the alarms, but didn't turn on the lights. They looked shocked. I think they were wearing their night clothes. There were three kids, including the boy, and strangers who were a little bit upset about something. I tried to find out what was happening. I went up and began nuzzling Michelle's ankle and asking what the dilly-q, but she was shaking and wide-eyed, like Annika gets in a thunderstorm.

One of the adults, a stranger called Rebecca, herded the kids into the front office while the other adults brought in sleeping bags and cardboard boxes from their vehicle. Jason had a hunting rifle that he held really tight and he kept looking around the parking lot while everyone else moved the boxes into the store.

When they were done, they locked the door and Michelle hung a curtain over it. I protested! How would people see inside? How would I greet them to my home?

But then Jason and Michelle moved a wooden counter in front of the door. I got nervous! What was going on? This was no way to share books with people! While that happened, a horrible scraping insulted my ears and I had to run over to the sunrise side windows

Squeekie vs. the Stinkie Apocalypse

by the road where all the vehicles passed to see three strangers throwing books onto the floor and pulling the wooden case away from its spot on the floor.

"Stop it," I squeaked. "Leave those books alone!"

I jumped up on the table where I spent valuable nap time and protested some more. One big man I didn't recognize – he had on a bright shirt covered in flames and motorcycles and had trimmed white face-fur in spots – turned the book case sideways and lifted it. I mean, it was huge! But the man lifted it and brought it toward me. Hands grabbed me and pulled me off the table so the book case could block the windows.

"What's going on," I asked even though I know perfectly well no human speaks Cat.

Except Andrew Lloyd Webber, of course, and he wasn't there to translate.

It was a long night.

Irving and Petunia usually get locked in the pen at night to avoid getting lost in the big, dark bookstore or getting into "mischief" among the bookshelves. That, night, though, Michelle let their pen open before joining the other grown up people in the back part of the store, beyond where customers are allowed to go.

Under portable lamps, they spoke in hushed tones about monsters on the streets and how they were going to get out of town and where they could escape because, as Eric said, "This is, like, everywhere."

Leave my home, I thought. *And go where?*

Michelle said no one else was coming because the bridges to Harrisburg were shut down or blocked by...something bad. Jason kept trying to use his cell phone, but he just kept shaking it like it did something wrong. Michelle, who always kept a clear head about things, said, "We have to admit no one else is meeting us here. We have to plan what's next and fast."

I slipped into the small break area up front where three kids whispered to one another about what they thought was happening. A young girl with black hair and glasses – *Shiny*, I think was her name – looked a little shaken up, so I rubbed my head on her leg and told her a joke, which didn't go over well because, as I mentioned, no one speaks cat. The other kids, including Michelle and Jason's kid, were talking about what they saw out on the street. When I walked by to find out what they were saying, they decided it was play time and I kinda lost track of everything with all the pets and the scratches and hugs.

But then Rebecca appeared in the doorway and scared me with a loud SHUSH. The kids were being too loud, she said. I ran out of the room and made my way to the window beside the street.

Tobor was there – did I mention Tobor? No? Well, she was there, sitting at the reading table and peeking out through a gap between the bookcase and the windowpane. Tobor was another rescue foster sibling, though she did her best to pretend not, was a young Russian Blue with a gunmetal gray coat and a secretive nature. She used to tour with a rock band until she escaped the lifestyle and lived on the streets a while.

"Hey, Tobes," I said. "You know what's going on?"

Tobor turned her head toward me, slow, and then fixed me with a blank stare. "The end is coming," she said like someone else would tell me it was a fine night for a walk. She had a thick, posh accent and used big words sometimes.

"The end of what?"

"The end of the world of men," she hissed. "Just like the prophets promised, Squeekie. The souls of the dead will not leave the bodies and so they walk, hunting and feeding on the living."

"Wow." I considered this a moment and then asked Tobor, "That's dark. How do you know all that?"

Tobor turned away from the window and settled down in front of me, wrapping her tail around her paws. She tilted her head to one side like she was deciding if she should bother explaining.

"It stinks outside," Captain Fabulous said as he hopped up on the table and poked his nose into a small gap in the bookcase. Cap Fab didn't seem bothered by the whole affair except that it stank. He hopped down from the desk to the chair where someone had moved a small bed, and curled up in it.

"The stories of felines passed down from the times of ancient Egypt," Tobor rasped. "The days when the dead would rise and cleanse the Great Kingdoms of people and grant control to the rightful Kings and Queens."

I dared ask, "Who dat?"

Squeekie vs. the Stinkie Apocalypse

Tobor's eyes narrowed. "Why, cats, of course. Not all cats...not you anyway. You're just a servant class housecat. But I will be a goddess to these creatures and rule as I should."

"Whatever, creepy. I'm sure that's an awesome story you tell the other cats on the bus to Metalpalooza or whatnot. Just don't tell that story to the kittens."

Tobor sniffed and hissed and spit. "The rotting flesh of the humans at the dawn of the End Times," Tobor growled at the window. I spotted movement along the railroad tracks across the street. There were a lot of people outside in the moonlight. No cars along the street. No lights at all, I realized. Just the moon and a bunch of people in the dark staggering and stumbling toward the book store.

Someone tapped on the front door of the store.

That brings me back to the dude at the start of my story.

There was a dude at the door. But that dude was not right.

It was the white, milky eyes that bugged me most.

We had this blind foster cat here once with the same look. But this dude kept looking toward the sound of my voice.

"Hey buddy," I said. "We're closed until tomorrow at ten, okay?"

When I paced from one side of the door to the other, he followed me.

"For serious, bro," I continued. "thanks for coming out, but it's a private thing we've got happening in here, okay?"

He reached down to the glass like he might be able to reach through and, when his fingers bumped against the door, he tried a few more times. I mean, humans can be dumb, but even the dumbest cat won't headbutt a plate glass window more than once. This dude kept slapping the glass to try and grab me.

I hissed and -whoah - he staggered back into a spot where the moonlight shone brighter on his whole body.

Dude was pale and wore the kind of clothes people on the railroad wear when they fix the tracks across the street; one gray jumpsuit that was torn up pretty bad. It was stained around the torn areas with dark red that soaked through the material. It explained why the man looked sick and pale, but it didn't explain the tangle of ivy around his chest and arms or the dead leaves stuck in his hair and clothes. If what he was saying was People language, it was out of words I never heard. He sounded more like a dog out of breath and still pulling against a leash.

"Dude," I said. "I think you need a people vet."

Shadows fell across the doorway and instinct made me jump across the barricade to the opposite side. I heard more of those gargling, hissing sounds that the odd dude made. Suddenly, there were four more sick-looking people at the door, each looking down at me with the same, blank expression and milky, white eyes. They growled like Annika does when she's both hungry AND cranky. They all tried to claw through the glass until one of them got the bright idea to wander off and return with a big rock from the parking lot.

That's when I decided it was time to run away and get a human person.

I was half the way between the entrance and the back-office camping spot area when the banging started. The sound was so loud that it brought the people running. I tried to get their attention as they rushed the door, but they just ran right by me toward the entrance, shouting at each other.

The pounding of rock on glass and metal continued. Every few hits came with the sick sound of cracking glass.

I made my way to the catwalk that runs around the upper part of the building and along the book shelves. A long ramp from the cash register led up to the main walkway that I take when there are too many people for me to deal. I'm not a big fan of the height, but it seemed like a good place to go at the time.

Passing Tobor, I heard her say "When there's no more room in Duat; the dead will walk the Earth."

"*Not. Helping.*" I ran by her and up the ramp. She sneezed and then giggled a bit before returning to her spot on the sunrise window.

The fosters Irving and Petunia were up in the catwalk nearest the ramp staring down in terror. Annika, as usual, lay below us on her bed beside the north side window looking bored. She kept staring out the gap in the wood planks across it and I shouted down,

"How many of those things are out there, Neek?"

She didn't answer at first. She yawned.

"Neek!"

She growled. "Whaaat?!"

"How many people are outside?"

"They is not peoples, stupid. They is…*dead*."

"Sorry, did you say 'dead'?"

"Yaaaaaas," she replied with that tone that suggested I was dumber than she. "Dead peoples walkin' 'round."

"Come on, Neek. You're not down with Tobor's 'End of Days' nonsense, too, are you?"

The kittens squealed. "End of Days?!"

"Dang it," I said under my squeak.

Tobor hissed in the direction of the front entrance. The people were shouting and suddenly the glass shattered.

"Shore up the barricade," Eric yelled. "Don't let them in! Watch their hands, Jason: they've got a GRIP."

A cloud of stink – worse than a spoiled litter box and old cat food combined – passed over us. Ugh, it was awful. It was coming from the front door.

Irving and Petunia huddled together in the shadows, mewing like kittens, puffed up like they were just fished out of a dryer. "What happening," Irving whined. "What do we do?"

"Stay calm," I said. We're up here. They can't get us. Let the people handle it. If it gets really bad..." I paused because I didn't want to think about the really bad.

Petunia insisted, "What, Squeek?"

"There's a secret exit in the basement we can use to get out."

"And go wheres, genius?"

It was Annika. She had jumped out of her bed by the high window and came strutting up the ramp to the landing.

"You can lead the little ones out."

She hissed. "First-o, you ain't the boss o'me. Second-o, what're you gonna do?"

"I'm gonna stay and help the people, our family."

She hissed like a deflating balloon. "What are *you* gonna do? They was eatin' dead birds and squirrels outside."

A sudden, loud CRUNCH of a wood and metal echoed through the store followed by Eric and Michelle screaming "Get it out of the door! Push it back!" Over their shouts, the sound of moaning grew louder and more desperate.

"Get 'em off me!" Eric sounded scared.

"Hold still!" Michelle yelled over the rising growls and groans. Irving and Petunia huddled up against me, crying as the sound of crushing glass and scraping metal continued followed by a terrible, roar that hit us all with a punch and made everything in the world ring. A wave of pressure pushed me backwards, but I steadied myself. I shook my head to clear the ringing, but it wouldn't go away.

That's when I saw Irving hanging by his claws on the catwalk, a long ways over the concrete floor – like *splat* distance high, terror in his eyes. Petunia was paralyzed with fear. Annika ran for the back half of the store and a better place to hide, her weight shaking the catwalk and making it hard to steady myself.

I turned around and lay on the catwalk, gripping the far side with my front paws and letting my butt and tail hang down over the other side. Hoping that the little guy could hear me, I cried, "Swing up and grab my butt, Irving! Grab my tail and get up here! Petunia help him!"

Irving's rear claws cut into my hide. I didn't want to, but I howled. Kitten claws are like razors but it was a good thing for Irving: the front claws held him to the walkway and the back claws gave him the leverage to climb back up to the catwalk.

Oh, it hurt. But Irving climbed over me and landed in a ball beside me, purring loud and panting. Petunia sniffed him over and started tonguing his coat at the top of his head.

The ringing had softened a bit and I could hear low, distorted sounds like the dead people moaning through the plate glass – but it was the humans talking. I winced as I turned myself around to see what was happening. My wounds pulled as I bent around but there were Michelle, Eric, and Rebecca around the corner from the entryway. They looked scared and tired... but relieved. With the doorway now a pile of heavy wood and metal, they moved the children back with them behind the curtains in the stock room.

I sniffed the air and scanned the sales floor "Where are Tobor and Captain Fabulous?"

It was at a point where I could hear myself mew, but the ringing persisted. The older cats were nowhere around. No doubt they were hiding and keeping away from the source of the lingering stench in the air.

"You guys stay up here and wait for me," I said. "If you hear me call – you come running. If not, stay until I get you." I didn't want to explain that if the people decided to leave, they'd go fast and I didn't want the kittens to hold everything up by making them search the building. On the other hand, that last break-in looked

Squeekie vs. the Stinkie Apocalypse

pretty bad so there might not be time for them to escape. If the stinkies got inside...

I don't know how humans interpret a cat's song. Often, they come running to see what's wrong. Sometimes they throw shoes or yell at us to shut up. Tobor's song silenced the night – even the stinkies outside. They stopped banging on barricades and windows. Tobor's song was equal parts beautiful and horrible. A rough people translation would be:

The power of men forever shed
On the night even Pharaohs dread
When from their graves will come the dead.
The underworld will shut its gate
The dead to hungry bodies, straight
to eat the living they now hate.

There was more, but it got lost in another shattering of glass and splintering of wood.

Before the people could act, the stinkies were inside the book store.

I looked up to the rafters to tell the cats to move to the back of the store – but they were gone. I called out to them, but then the stinkies were past the atrium and in the main aisle.

Tobor was right there to greet them.

She stepped out of the book stacks and sat down about five feet from the first stinkie to appear. It looked like a police officer who rolled down a very big hill and that very big hill was covered in sharp rocks, spikes and razor wire. It focused on Tobor

"Welcome, my children," Tobor sang. "Let us begin the cleansing."

A stinkie in a Batman t-shirt and torn jeans staggered into sight followed by a woman with most of her insides on her outsides. She looked like Annika after a bath, all soggy with hair matted down, pale and milky-eyed like all the others. They looked at Tobor and all three moved toward her.

I didn't say anything as the three knelt and reached for her. I kept an eye on an escape route and any sign of the kittens. Other stinkies were wandering in and surrounding Tobor. She sat there confident and proud, tail wrapped around her paws like that statue she probably imagined would stand for her one day.

The police officer reached out and took Tobor into its grasp, gently and lovingly rising to its feet to turn and share her with the

Batman fan and the soggy lady. The short woman in a slick, red cocktail dress joined them in petting and squeezing Tobor. Tobor purred.

But then...

The stinkies hissed. I turned away, hoping that Tobor wasn't so drunk on her weird religion that she didn't see the small gap below her that might let her escape their clawing hands and gnashing jaws.

Whatever happened, I needed to make sure it didn't happen to the rest of us.

Suddenly the people burst out of the stock room with weapons, charging the stinkies with their rifles, a lamp pole, a hat rack, and a baseball bat. All the grown-ups were there except Rebecca who I imagine was watching over the kids.

When the stock room curtain parted, I saw something else that made my heart lighten a bit:

Annika.

That beautiful, grumpy, bitter, old so-and-so. She had the kittens safely off the sales floor and was herding them to the secret escape hatch.

Five of the rotten baddies turned the corner from the entryway into the main aisle joining the first three. The people spread out with their implements of destruction. With new confidence, I parked my fanny at the center of the Yellow Brick Road spiral and greeted them.

"Hello, stinkies! Welcome to my house. Get out before I kick you out."

They reached toward me and began to stoop to snatch me up, intending to tear me apart between them. I fought the instinct to run. They were still pretty far away, but the groaning and the gagging and the gnashing of teeth made it hard to hold my position. I just needed a few more seconds.

"HEY YEAH!" Captain Fabulous peeked out from atop the end cap full of mystery books, hissing and taunting the things. It slowed them down as they tried to work out which of us was the easiest prey.

I caught a scent in the air from behind me. Somehow the first creeps that got inside made their way around the back of the stacks and had me blocked in from behind! Three of the ghouls with only five legs between them staggered out from the kid books and

Squeekie vs. the Stinkie Apocalypse

literally fell over themselves trying to get at me. They tumbled to the floor, hands outstretched and clawing at me. I had to bolt for the stacks again but one of the ghouls blocked my way. I had to leap over one's head and dodge a swipe of another's hand, but I made it over them just as the newer group merged with them and they fumbled over one another trying to shoulder their way down the stacks after me.

Cap Fab paced the top of the stacks, howling and humming until two of the ghouls grabbed the end cap and shook it hard. The old cat slipped and tumbled, falling from the top of the stack and disappearing into the crowd with a frightened howl.

I sprinted toward a gap in the books at the bottom of one stack and squeezed through another tight hole between hardback fiction. The left was blocked by two ghouls fighting over stingy remains of something – or someone – but the right way was clear. Unfortunately, it took me back in the direction of the larger mob. I turned to hide back in the stacks just in time to see a gray hand rip through the gap and grab my tail. The grip was so strong, I howled and rolled over onto my back trying to break free. My claws scratched at the concrete as the hand pulled me back toward the shelves. The two stinkies at the end of the aisle saw me and lurched toward me. A pair of dead-eyed stinkies rounded the other end of the aisle.

In any other situation, I would have curled back around and, before the thought crossed my mind, bit into the hand hurting me. But something about that flesh, those bodies, cancelled my instinct. I slashed at the flesh but it didn't respond. I cut deep, but the wounds didn't bleed.

Shadows loomed as the other stinkies closed in around me.

Panic, panic, panic! I dug into the spines of books to keep from getting pulled into the darkness but I fell through and away from the stinkies lunging at me in the aisle. In the dark, I could hear the gnashing of teeth and snarling of the things that probably ate up old Cap Fab. I made confetti out of Raymond Chandler and Raymond Chambers books. The pain made me fight and claw and scrape as I fell backward through the hole...

And then the hand let go.

Terrible crunching sounds, like a folding chair landing in a tub of wet tuna delight. Horrible groans and gurgles. A heavy thud and wet thumps of slip across cement. And the aisle behind me went quiet.

I curled up in a ball inside that dark space. My tail ached and my butt throbbed from where Irving dug into it. I thought about poor Cap Fab falling into that mob. There was no way he could have gotten away, was there?

I didn't even see the guy kneeling, looking into the hole at me.

Not a stinkie.

It was the one called Eric – the big man in the shirt covered in fire and motorcycles. "Hey," he said in a hushed voice. "It's okay. We're getting out. Come on."

I wasn't moving. Even as the sounds of crushing and crunching and bashing silenced the growls and snarls on the other side of the stack, I wasn't going anywhere. Too close. Too close to getting snacked on by stinkies.

"Come on, Squeeks," Eric said. "Your family needs you."

That got through to me. Annika, that pain in the butt, was outside with Irving and Petunia. They got out and they'll need me, I thought. Annika was not an outdoor cat.

But I was still scared.

"But what about the stinkies," I whined at Eric.

"Come on," he said. "I'm too big to get in there and get you out."

"That's kinda the point, friend-o."

His round, friendly face stayed in the gap, a small mag light reminding me he was one of the good people.

Someone yelled off to one side. "Are we clear through Science Fiction?"

Another voice called back "I'm all the way in Westerns. We're gold over here. I got Captain Fabulous!"

A warm feeling flushed my shaky bits away at that news.

"Is he okay," I heard Michelle ask.

"Found him trying to claw his way into the catnip box, so...yeah."

Carefully, I creeped from my space in the dark toward Eric and emerged among a pile of silent and limp stinkies. I struggled a bit when Eric grabbed me, but settled down when he put me on his shoulder. "Come with me if you wan'to live," he mumbled and then chuckled to himself. "I always wanted to say that."

Squeekie vs. the Stinkie Apocalypse

All those stinkie people. It was beyond me what happened to them. Eric carried me back to where everyone had been hiding behind walls of hardback books. Eric handed me off to Eric's little kid – Shiny – who noticed the blood on my back and told her mom. Michelle brought a first aid kit over in one hand with Captain Fabulous under her other arm. He looked zonkered on the nip. I wish I had been.

"Dude," Cap Fab said as Michelle put him down next to me on the desk. "Did you see that action, man? It was <u>freaky</u>, man."

"Freaky, sure." I sneezed and started grooming myself to calm my nerves. "Any sign of Tobor?"

"Nope." Cap Fab stretched and rolled onto his back inviting anyone and everyone to enjoy his soft ample belly. Unfortunately for him, I was the one getting all the attention.

Shiny gave awesome pets and her mom and Michelle did their people magic to make the hurt in my butt and tail go away a little before wrapping me in this annoying white ribbon. I know why they did it, but that didn't make me like it.

"What about the other cats," Michelle asked somebody I couldn't see. I wanted to tell her about Annika and the kittens so she didn't worry, but there wasn't much I could do to share. When I felt a little better – had some water and a good tongue bath – I'd head out the secret entrance and try to find them.

"Here they come," Jason called from his spot near the front window.

I didn't know what to make of that and tensed up.

Rapid pops and burps erupted outside and the night lit up with lightning flashes that set my fur on edge. Big rumbling machines and crunching gravel introduced something new outside my house.

"The trucks are coming into the lot," Jason said with a big grin. "Get everybody together!"

Everyone in the place scrambled to gather packs and their bedrolls, gather up boxes with people food and my cat stuff.

Eric's friend Rebecca dropped one of the travel prisons on the desk and said, "Sorry guys. You'll be traveling together for a while."

She opened the small metal gate in the side of the prison and both Cap and I did what we always do when we see it:

Nothing. No way do we travel in those things and certainly not two in one.

Sadly, big hands and quicker reflexes prevailed and we found ourselves stuffed into the prison before we knew it.

But I was too tired to care. Shiny peeped into our prison. She looked as tired as everyone else, but in much brighter spirits. She giggled at how weird we looked stuffed in a box. "It's okay," she said. "We're going to a safe place."

"Do they have nip," Cap asked without a reply.

Traveling by prison is disorienting even when I'm alone. I rarely go outside anymore. Cap and I bumped and rolled against one another as we were carried in a line from the back room to the front of the store. The door was wide open and a bright light made it hard to see what was beyond. We stepped over the stinkie piles and out into the fresh, cool air of the night. The rumbling sound came from big green trucks filling the lot. Some of them had guns at the top and others carried boxes and other people.

An older man in a green and gray uniform, white hair and ice-blue eyes stepped up to our spot in the line, grinning ear to ear at us. He looked at Rebecca, who was holding us, and said, "I'm Major Grant of the United States Army – on behalf of what's left of the United States I am happy to declare you well and truly rescued. And look here! I am such a cat person." He beamed at us. He seemed like such a nice man. He called off to one side. "Sergeant Wake! Put those 'dorbs up in the scout car with me and McInnes. Get 'em fed while we load up."

We said goodbye to the Cupboard Maker Book store one last time. Someone asked if people would ever buy books again. I wondered if I'd ever have such a wonderful home again. We were headed north, I heard one of the soldiers say, to a place with lots of people and even some animals.

We ended up in the back of a long, black SUV. From that per, I watched Michelle and her family load into the back of a truck and Eric's family load into another. Cap kept pressing against my ailing backside and I fought the urge to scratch at him. It wasn't his fault he was big and derpy.

But...I'm just a cat, y'know?

AUTHOR BIOGRAPHY

Jay Smith is an author and award-winning audio dramatist responsible for the Parsec Award-winning horror series **HG World**, the Parsec finalist **The Diary of Jill Woodbine** as well as the pulp adventure serial **Hidden Harbor Mysteries**. Jay's books include the gamer-geek satire **Rise of the Monkey Lord** and the novelization of The Diary of Jill Woodbine. His latest novel is the geek noir thriller **The Resurrection Pact**. Jay holds a Master of Fine Arts from Seton Hill University and is a member of the Horror Writers Association. jaysmithaudio.com

Squeekie the Bookstore Cat

12

The Drunken Comic Book Monkeys vs. Squeekie

Brian Koscienski & Chris Pisano

"Do you guys even know why you're here?"

"Bacon," Brian replied.

"Bacon," Chris answered.

Michelle, the well-respected owner of Cupboard Maker Books, slapped her palm against her forehead. She ran her hand down her face as if trying to pull all the bad thoughts out of her head. "Seriously? The event is called Books, Bonding, and Bacon, remember? You guys set up a table for your books and you bond with the community."

"Bacon," Chris said.

"Community?" Brian asked.

Michelle sighed. "Yes, community. You know – neighbors. People. Camaraderie. Socially acceptable human interaction."

Brian and Chris looked at each other as if Michelle spoke to them in a foreign language. They shrugged and looked back at Michelle with lost puppy-dog eyes.

"Did you idiots at least bring books?"

Brian held out a dozen copies of *The Drunken Comic Book Monkeys in: Scary Tales of Scariness* while Chris presented twelve copies of *The Drunken Comic Book Monkeys in: Sciencey Tales of Science Fiction.*

Brow flattened and lips pursed, Michelle mumbled, "You guys think you're so meta, don't you?"

"We try," Brian said.

"Bacon," Chris said.

"Fine!" Michelle snapped. "I'll go start the bacon. It'll be done in ten minutes, so stay out of trouble." She rolled her eyes and stormed off in a huff.

Putting their books on the table, Brian said, "This is why she likes me more."

Chris fussed with the books, trying to arrange them in a pleasant display. "Why? Because I'm succinct and don't waste her valuable time with superfluous hyperbole? I'm not a sesquipedalian individual like you."

"Yeah, that's me. Using big words for no reason at all. Yep, totally me," Brian replied, sarcasm dripping from his words. Noticing a small puddle forming on the corner of the tablecloth, he realized it wasn't truly sarcasm dripping from him, but rather the thoughts of bacon kicking his saliva glands into high gear.

In an effort to hide the drool spot, he shifted the tablecloth and caused the stacks of books to move an inch and a half. This, of course, rankled Chris. "Dude! You moved the books that I've been working hard to arrange in a pleasant display."

"Yeah? Well, this is how Squeekie wants them."

"Squeekie? What are you even talking about?"

As if on cue, Squeekie, the guardian lion of the store (in Siamese cat form, that is) jumped onto the table and rubbed against one of the stacks, knocking it over creating a festive fanning effect with the books. Brian gestured to Squeekie with both hands and said, "See? Squeekie wants it this way."

"I highly doubt that."

Squeekie meowed.

Brian leaned close to Chris and attempted to whisper, but it came out more like a yell, "I think Squeekie is after our bacon."

Chris waved his hands about as if shooing away an insect. "You're louder than an erupting volcano, and twice as terrifying. Of course Squeekie wants our bacon. He's a cat and cats love bacon. But he's not getting any of mine."

"Well, he's not getting of mine, either, unless he finds a way to distract us."

The cat meowed again and then jumped from the table. Confused, Brian and Chris followed Squeekie as he weaved his way among the shelves of the bookstore. Finally reaching the far corner of the store, Squeekie walked under a small archway covered with brush bristles, making sure they brushed the entire length of his back and tail. Purring, he turned around and repeated the process.

"A backscratcher. Why would he show us a backscratcher?" Chris asked. "Do you think he wants us to pet him?"

The Drunken Comic Book Monkeys vs. Squeekie

"Dude, you know very well that no living creature wants us to touch them. I think he's just showing off that he has cool toys and we don't."

"Well, that's mean."

"Yeah." Brian started to pout as he looked around, trying to determine if he could turn any part of the store into an ersatz backscratcher. He then found something better. "Oooooh, look at this."

"It's one of Squeekie's walkways."

Brian ran to the plank of wood spanning from the top of one bookshelf to another. "It is, but the bottom of it is line with some kind of felt or velvet."

"Felvet?"

"Exactly!"

"So?"

"Watch!" Brian ducked down and positioned himself under the walkway. Carefully, he stood until his head touched the felvet. Still crouched, he walked the length of the board, from one set of shelves to the other, his head sliding along the felvet. "Oooooh, that feels so good against my bald head."

"Hey! I have a bald head, too! I wanna try."

"You're too short."

"No I'm not!" Determined to prove his writing partner wrong, Chris positioned himself under the walkway and stood on his toes. Flapping his arms to keep his balance, he wobbled from one end of the walkway to the other, his head barely grazing along the felvet. "See? I can touch! I'm tall enough to ride this ride!"

"You're not doing it right! This is how you do it." Brian did another lap of gliding his head against the felvet.

Chris took exception and repeated the process, still flapping. "I'm faster!"

The men continued to run back and forth, slapping each other as they went along.

"I'm smarter!"

"I'm more elegant!"

"I'm better!"

"I'm prettier!"

One slap too many, the men knocked each other off balance, and both crashed into one of the shelves, knocking the walkway to the ground.

113

The two stood and stared at their mess, befuddled at how it came to be. Before they could burst into argument, Squeekie meowed to get their attention. The cat led and they blindly followed, all the way back to the front of the store. Once there, Squeekie walked around the counter. After a few seconds, a small ball – plastic and filled with tiny, aromatic leaves – rolled along the floor from behind the counter. Brian picked it up and sniffed it.

"Eeeeeew!" Chris crinkled his nose and furrowed his brows. "Do you always randomly sniff mysterious cat toys?"

Brian inhaled again. "I do when they're filled with hops."

"Hops! I wanna sniff!" Chris reached for the ball. Brian pulled it away, but having the coordination of a one-legged giraffe, he dropped it. Both men watched as the ball rolled down an aisle of books.

"Mine!" Brian yelled as he launched his flabby, out-of-shape body after it.

"Mine!" Chris lunged for the ball as well, body equally flabby and out-of-shape, just shorter.

Scrabbling along the ground, the men bounced from one shelf to the other while swatting at the ball. They gained and lost ground equally, the ball rolling sadistically just out of their reach. Brian elbowed Chris in the shoulder as they turned one corner; Chris kneed Brian in the hip when they turned the next corner. Alas, neither man could claim to be the victor as the ball rolled under one of the large shelves.

"Where's the ball go?" Chris asked, huffing and puffing on his hands and knees.

Panting, laying on his side, Brian answered, "Under the shelf there. Right where the red dot is."

"This red dot?" As Chris pointed to it, the little red dot moved a foot to the right. He aimed his index finger at it again, but it moved another foot to the right. "Hey! Why does it keep moving?"

"I don't know," Brian answered. "Hit it."

Chris tried. He slapped his hand on the floor where the red dot had been, missing as it jumped three feet to the left.

"You suck at this," Brian said as we strode over to the red dot and stepped on it. "See how easy that was?"

He missed as well, the dot now mere inches from his foot.

The Drunken Comic Book Monkeys vs. Squeekie

Chris stood and elbowed Brian out of the way. Putting the full weight of his body into it, he brought his foot down on the dot. "Here, I got this."

He did not get the dot. Both men watched as the dot danced in small circles while it made its way up the wall. Once the dot reached eye level, Chris swung after it, but missed. The dot now moved horizontally across the wall, avoiding Brian's hands with ease. Chris tried smacking at it again, but the red dot continued to move. Without warning, the dot went in the opposite direction, skimming along the wall even faster than before. Trying to anticipate its movements, Chris slapped both hands on the wall to no avail. Eyes widening with anticipation, Brian timed his hits perfectly, yet somehow still missed. Then the dot moved further up the wall.

Chris jumped and used both hands to swat at it. Even Brian had to stand on his toes to reach it. The dot angled downward, moving even faster than before. Whack, whack, Chris hit the wall with his hands. Smack, smack, Brian followed. Almost as if feeding off the men's collective incompetence, the elusive dot picked up speed.

Whack, whack.
Smack, smack.
Miss, miss.

The men moved apart, Brian claiming the left side of the wall while Chris guarded the right. In big looping circles, the dot scooted from one side of the wall to the other.

Whack, whack.
Smack, smack.
Miss, miss.

Panting and sweating, the men pawed at the dot whenever it got close to them, watched with rapt fascination whenever it was away from them. Their attacks became more frenzied, their hits more intense. Finally, the dot stopped moving. Right between the two men.

They released a battle cry and pounced, a furious attempt to stop the madness. The madness did end – with the hollow coconut sound of two empty heads colliding. The men slid down the wall, finishing in an unconscious heap of stupidity.

Michelle walked around the corner with a tray of bacon in her hands. "Okay, guys, I have your—" She cut herself short when she noticed the mess on the floor. "What have you two morons done this time?"

No answer.

She sighed, the involuntary reaction to the frustration of dealing with Brian and Chris, and walked to the front of the store to find Squeekie sitting on the checkout counter with a laser pointer in his mouth. Smiling, Michelle set the bacon on the counter and took the laser pointer. Petting him, Michelle said, "What are you doing with this thing? Oh well, I made bacon for the guys, but it doesn't seem like they want any, so it's all yours."

Squeekie purred.

Life was good.

The Drunken Comic Book Monkeys vs. Squeekie

AUTHOR BIOGRAPHY

Brian Koscienski & Chris Pisano skulk the realms of south, central Pennsylvania. Brian developed a love of writing from countless hours of reading comic books and losing himself in the worlds and adventures found within their colorful pages. In tenth grade, Chris was discouraged by his English teacher from reading H.P. Lovecraft, and being a naturally disobedient youth he has been a fan ever since. They have logged many hours writing novels, stories, articles, comic books, reviews, and the occasional bawdy haiku. During their tenure as a writing duo, they even started Fortress Publishing, Inc., a micro-press publishing company responsible for the *Drunken Comic Book Monkeys* short story collections and the *TV Gods* anthologies.

Squeekie the Bookstore Cat

13

Everybody Needs a Friend

Carrie Jacobs

Friendship. To Squeekie, it was one of the most important things in the world. He made it his life's mission – all nine of his lives' mission – to befriend all the rescue kitties who came through the book store doors, and help connect them with new human friends. He adored his kitty friends, especially grumpy Annika, and he loved his human friends.

He loved watching human friends come into the bookstore together, pointing out favorite books, helping each other discover new worlds between the pages, and becoming even better friends in the process.

Because he loved friendship so much, his ears perked up when he heard two ladies talking. Squeekie had been napping behind the radio, high above the large-print section, when the ladies sat down at the table, taking a break from browsing.

"Oh, Lois, I don't know what to do. Emma just doesn't seem to be making any friends," one of the women said. Her voice was sad.

Squeekie wanted to jump down and give her a head boop. Those always made the humans feel better. But he stayed where he was and listened.

The woman continued. "She's always got her nose in a book."

The second woman chuckled. "She got that from you, you know."

"It skipped a generation. My daughter hardly reads at all. I'm glad Emma likes to read, but she needs some real friends."

"It must be hard on her, moving in with her grandma while her parents travel the world. Especially in the middle of the school year," the second woman said kindly.

"It is. It's worse since her brother is a social butterfly. He had new friends the first day."

"She'll find her place, Sue. Just be patient."

Squeekie had never met Emma, but he felt bad for her. He peeked over the wall, hoping to catch a glimpse of the ladies. His eyes widened with recognition. They were both regular customers. He got up and stretched, then took the short way to the front counter. He had an idea.

Squeekie was on a mission. He landed on the counter with a soft "thud" and nudged a stack of papers until it fell over, spreading the pages across the counter.

Annika poked her head out of the basket she had been napping in. "What are you doing?"

"Looking for someth- here it is!" He placed his paw on the paper and pulled it free from the scattered stack.

The ladies arrived and placed their stacks of books on the well-loved wooden counter. Sue patted Squeekie's head. He tapped the paper with his paw. "Here! Give this to Emma," he said.

Annika snickered.

Sue kept petting him, but didn't look at the paper.

"Look. At. This." Squeekie spoke slowly, carefully enunciating his words.

"Ooh yes, you's such a good kitty, isn't you?"

Annika rocked the basket with her laughter. "You know they don't understand you, Squeekie. You give people way, way too much credit."

"Help me, Annika, this is important!"

With an inconvenienced sigh, Annika gracefully jumped out of the basket and stretched. She tiptoed over to the counter. "What are we doing?"

"She needs to see this." He tapped the paper.

Annika cocked her head. "I'll try." She hunched her shoulders and started making an awful horfing noise.

"What are you doing?!"

Horf! Horf! Horf!

The hairball landed in the exact middle of the page. Annika grinned at her handiwork. "You're welcome."

Squeekie stared at the blob in horror. "Oh no, you've ruined it!"

"Poor kitty," Lois said, reaching out to pet Annika, who narrowed her eyes in warning. The woman paid no attention, and was rewarded with a small scratch to the back of her hand.

Annika jumped to the floor. "Well, I tried."

Squeekie sighed. "Thanks, I think."

"Eew." Michelle threw the paper in the trash and scratched Squeekie's head. He looked around, trying to find something else that might work. There was nothing.

The women paid for their books and put them in their canvas store bags. Squeekie watched Michelle drop two nickels into the can beside the register. "Since you brought your own bags, the rescue gets a nickel for each of you."

Sue smiled. "Here's another dollar for the can. It's such a good cause."

"I have something important to tell you," Squeekie yelled at Sue.

"Oh yes, you're such a talkative little fellow, aren't you? I'll bring some treats for you and your friends next week."

"Bring Emma with you," he pleaded.

She scratched his chin and baby-talked to him. "You's such a good boy. Such a sweet widdle boy. Yesh you is."

Exasperated, Squeekie turned and walked across the counter, stepped onto the cash register, then jumped up onto one of the cat perches and made his way to the top of the shelves, where Annika was hiding.

"I don't know why they insist on talking to me like that. I'm highly educated. For Pete's sake, I live in a *bookstore*."

Annika's eyes widened in surprise. "You sound upset. That's not like you."

Squeekie tucked his paws under his belly and settled himself down, wrapping his tail around his side. "I feel bad for Emma. She doesn't have any friends. Everybody needs friends. Even you."

Annika thrust her back leg out and licked it. "I suppose you're right. What's the plan?"

Squeekie shook his head. "I'm going to sleep on it."

"Good idea. I'll join you." She curled up and purred them both to sleep.

Squeekie had just gotten comfortable in his hiding spot, away from a rambunctious new tuxedo kitten, when a familiar voice made him perk up.

He listened closely. It had to be Sue.

"This is the bookstore I was telling you about, Emma."

"Wow, Grandma, this is awesome."

"Go look around. Try to stay under budget."

Squeekie peeked around the corner, trying to catch a glimpse of Emma. He trotted toward the YA section at the back of the store. He scurried around the corner, coming face to face with a well-worn pair of pink Converse sneakers. He looked up into a pretty face framed with long brown hair. Her bright blue eyes crinkled at the edges, behind black framed glasses, as she smiled at him. She hunkered down. "Hi, kitty."

Squeekie gave her his best purr and wound around her legs, wrapping his tail around her ankle.

Emma scratched Squeekie's head. "You're such a pretty kitty. So friendly."

"What about me?" The new kitten bounced over, jumping and spinning, his tiny tail straight up in the air, his eyes wide and excited. He pounced at the fingers Emma was wiggling at him. "What about me? Am I pretty? I think you're pretty. You have a lot of strings. I love strings."

Squeekie chuckled. "Simmer down, Sammy, humans can't understand us when we talk."

"How come? Why not? That's silly. We can understand them, so how come they can't understand us? Huh, Squeekie? How come?" Sammy was attacking Emma's shoelaces while he talked a mile a minute.

"Sammy, let's go so Emma can look for some books."

"Aww, do we hafta?"

Squeekie nodded.

"Fiiiiine," Sammy gave Emma's shoelace one last swat and darted away.

Emma laughed as she watched him go. Satisfied, Squeekie rubbed against her leg and walked away. He stayed close, though, peeking at her through the aisles, listening to her hum. He liked her voice. She seemed happy, browsing the aisles, reading the backs of books and making a stack on the front counter, but Squeekie knew her grandmother was right. Emma needed some friends.

Ones that lived outside the pages of a book.

Emma picked up a book and flipped through the pages. She added it to her pile. Squeekie watched her stand and wrestle with the stack of books. She carried them to the front of the store, where her grandmother was chatting with Michelle.

Everybody Needs a Friend

Squeekie jumped up on the counter and rubbed against Emma's stack of books. He purred while she scratched his head.

"Have you read the Study series by Maria V. Snyder?" Michelle was asking Emma.

"No, what are they about?"

Squeekie sat down while Michelle raved about the series. "Maria's amazing. And she's going to be here for a book signing next weekend."

Michelle slid a flyer across the counter and Squeekie pounced on it, meowing loudly. He took another step to a pile of flyers and stepped on the one he wanted. "Give her this, too!" He kneaded the paper, crinkling the corner.

"Good idea, Squeekie, you're so smart." Michelle scratched his chin and handed an un-kneaded paper to Emma. "We also have a Teen Book Club, if you're interested."

Squeekie head booped Emma's hand and gave a loud meow.

Emma laughed. "Looks like Squeekie wants me to sign up."

He purred and rubbed his cheek on her hand.

Sue patted her granddaughter's shoulder. "That sounds wonderful."

"Here's the current book they're reading." Michelle handed her a copy to look at.

Emma smiled. "I've actually been wanting to read that." She added the book to her pile, along with a copy of Poison Study.

"We should get going, we have to pick your brother up." Sue paid for their books and put them in her canvas store bag while Michelle dropped a nickel into the can.

Emma nodded and folded both flyers and stuck them in the pocket of her jeans. "Maybe I'll see you next week," she said to Squeekie.

"I hope so," he said, knowing she only heard him meow.

Squeekie watched her push the glass door open and leave the store. He curled up on the counter.

"Was that your genius plan?" Annika poked her head over the basket.

"Yep."

Annika gave him an approving nod. "Not bad."

The next weekend, Squeekie scampered to and fro, showing off his new bow tie, carrying out his host duties for Maria's book signing. The door opened a hundred times, customers and fans filling the store and lining up to have their books autographed.

Squeekie shook his head at Annika, who was perched on the windowsill in the foyer, wanting everyone to fuss over how pretty she was, but not touch her. Annika nodded her head toward the door. "Here she comes."

The door opened and Emma and her grandmother walked in. Squeekie ran over and rubbed against Emma's leg. She petted him, then followed her grandmother to the counter, where they purchased the rest of the books in the Study series.

Emma got in line to have her books autographed.

Squeekie grinned when he saw another girl about her age get in line right behind her. "Come on, come on, start a conversation."

"Have you read any of them?" The blonde girl asked Emma.

"Yessss!" Squeekie did a little bounce.

Emma turned. "Me?"

"You're Emma, right?"

"Yeah. Yes. I just read the first one. I'm sorry, I just moved here and I'm not sure what your name is."

"Cassidy. We have chem together. Where'd you move from?"

"Colorado. I'm living with my grandmother."

"Me, too." Cassidy laughed. "*My* grandmother, not yours. So you liked Poison Study?"

"Ohmigosh, I couldn't put it down. I can't wait to read the rest of the series."

Squeekie watched the girls for a few minutes, then went to mingle with the crowd. When he came back, they were giggling and talking like they'd known each other for years.

"You should come to the book club," Cassidy was saying.

"I might. I started the book you guys are reading, but I haven't finished it yet."

"Once you hit the middle, you won't be able to put it down. You'll definitely have it done before the next meeting. Let me get your number." Cassidy pulled out her cell phone.

Emma pulled hers out, too, and they exchanged numbers.

"I'll add you to my Goodreads, too."

"Awesome," Emma answered.

Squeekie was rather pleased with his success. He straightened his bowtie and went off to enjoy the rest of the party, hoping someone would drop a piece of cake so he could clean up their icing.

Everybody Needs a Friend

He kept an eye on Emma and Cassidy. They chatted until they reached Maria's table and got their books signed.

Squeekie had to laugh. When Emma reached Maria, she got tongue-tied and star-struck. Cassidy nudged her arm and whispered, "She's super nice. Relax."

He watched as they left the signing table and stuck together, both of them talking incessantly.

A few days later, Squeekie and Annika sat side by side on top of one of the bookshelves, watching the nine teenagers laugh and talk and discuss books. Emma exchanged numbers with everyone in the group.

"Did you hear the good news?" Squeekie asked. "Sammy got his forever home. Emma's grandma adopted him. He's going home with them tonight after book club."

"That's wonderful," Annika said, swishing her fluffy tail. Sammy was under the table, attacking Emma's shoestrings. "She really seems to fit in."

Squeekie nodded. "I'm so glad."

"Me, too. I know what it's like to be uprooted from the only home you've ever known and get dropped in a strange place. It's not easy."

Squeekie settled onto his belly, remembering how frightened Annika was when she'd arrived at the bookstore. He watched the kids clean up their books and paper and smiled as Emma scooped Sammy up and kissed his head.

Sammy wriggled and caught the string of her hoodie in his mouth. He caught Squeekie's eyes and grinned. "Bye, Squeekie! Bye, Annika! I'm going home with Emma!" he mewed.

Squeekie waved good-bye to him. "Your story has a happy ending, too, Annika."

"Only thanks to you. If you ever tell anyone I said this, I'll deny it. But you're right. Everyone needs a good friend. Even me." She yawned. "I'm glad you're my best friend."

Squeekie started to answer, but Annika was already pretending to be asleep. He leaned over and gave her a light head boop. "Me, too."

Carrie Jacobs

AUTHOR BIOGRAPHY

Carrie Jacobs began her writing career at age three, when, still lacking the dexterity to form recognizable letters, she dictated a riveting tale to her transcriptionist, AKA Mom. "A Frog Named Tog" rocketed to #1 in the family, but did not garner international acclaim. It did, however, serve as an early clue that writing would be a lifelong journey.

Since then, she spent approximately fifteen years as a columnist for a local weekly newspaper, writing "slice of life" type articles. She also frequently write articles for a local non-profit. Carrie has won two first-place awards through Pennwriters.

She loves writing contemporary romance novels, and writes short stories in any genre imaginable, including the weird and creepy. Her settings are many places she's visited and her hometown, all thrown into a blender and poured out into the place she would most love to live. Her characters are people she knows, would like to know, or would like to avoid.

Carrie lives in beautiful central Pennsylvania with her family and spoiled pets.

Connect with her on Facebook at facebook.com/writercarriejacobs, on Twitter at @carrieinpa or on her website at carrieajacobs.com.

14

Squeekie Saves the Store

Natalie J. Damschroder

"Night, Squeekie. See you in the morning!"

The lock snicked and the door rattled as the human tested it. Feet crunched as they walked away, and Squeekie's ears flicked, listening for the rumble that meant they weren't coming back inside for something they forgot. Then that, too, faded, and all was silent.

And Squeekie went to work. He padded silently down the last row of bookstacks, ensuring all was in its place, peaceful. He was Adventure Cat, on the prowl, prepared to defend and protect. Down the back wall, with a pause to nod at Bob the Bookstore Ghost, out for a stroll. Or a glide, since his feet didn't move.

He was halfway up the first row when the door rattled. He froze, concentrating. Scraping noises came from the front of the store, and a harsh voice, muffled too much to understand the words, reached his ears.

He scrambled—no, *dashed* to the front of the store and up the best route to the top of the shelves next to the counter, where he could see whoever was coming in but could hide in the shadows. The voices were clearer now, using the kinds of words and tone he rarely heard in the store. These were men, angry men, and they did not belong here.

The door opened. With a scuffle, two men came in. They wore what the no-longer-small human called hoodies, so Squeekie couldn't see their faces. He had never seen—or smelled—them before. A strange odor tickled his nose, and he pawed it to keep from sneezing and giving away his position. He had the advantage, the high ground, like the Navy SEALs in those books, and he wasn't giving way.

"Hurry and get away from the door!" one of the men said. The other one turned the lock and they backed hurriedly out of the foyer. They stood, watching the entrance, panting like stupid dogs for a few seconds. In the cage next to them, the two young cats (Squeekie forgot their names, since they'd only been here two days and he never bothered to learn them for at least a week) stood and meowed. One purred, the attention hog, and the shorter guy flipped back his hood and leaned down, smiling, the light from the parking lot showing broken teeth.

"Hey, little one. Ain't you just the cutest."

"Leave it alone." The bigger guy shoved past him and turned, tapping his thumb and pinky against his thigh, back and forth, back and forth, really fast, Squeekie could catch it, could pounce and stop it...

He was crouching. He shook off the instinct and settled into a low stance, as if he'd meant to shift his position all along.

Short Guy straightened, the smile going away. "How long you think we gotta wait?"

"A while. Maybe morning."

No way. Squeekie knew these guys were bad. It was instinct, which, as Adventure Cat, he had more of than the usual kitty. They reeked of desperation, like a lot of the cats did when they came in here from really bad places. Those cats got love and food and protection and found good homes. These men would just get more desperate. And that meant if Squeekie's humans showed up in the morning, *this* could become a bad place.

Big Guy eyed the space behind the counter, then walked around the favorites rack and over to the button machine. "Think they keep money in here overnight?"

Short Guy didn't answer, and Big Guy started pushing buttons. Squeekie had to stop him. Mother was always in a really bad mood if anything happened with the green paper. He had to stop Big Guy. He yowled and leaped, landing on his head, claws digging in to the hoodie and the scalp beneath.

He had really good claws.

The man screamed and spun. Squeekie held on as he staggered around, knocking over stacks of books. Big Guy finally got his hands around Squeekie's middle and flung him off. Squeekie hit the ground running, streaking around the corner well ahead of the clunky, thunking boots behind him.

Squeekie Saves the Store

"Get that cat!" Big Guy yelled, but Squeekie ducked under a shelf and stilled.

"Where is he?" the man bellowed.

"Where's who?" Short Guy asked, as if he hadn't seen what just happened.

Squeekie stifled a purr of satisfaction. These guys were dumb. This would be easy. He stayed where he was, letting the men stomp around looking for him for a few minutes.

Eventually, Short Guy said, "I gotta take a leak."

Squeekie knew what that meant. He slunk out of his hiding spot and glided behind the shelves to the back of the store, while Short Guy stomped around some more, looking for the room with the whirlpool fountain. When he found it and slammed the door, Squeekie made his move. Next to the door was a tall rack of paperback books. He knew just the right angle to knock it over. He'd done it before. This time would be on purpose.

In a few leaps he was on top of a tall shelf. He wiggled his feet under himself just right, stared at the place he needed to land, and jumped. All four feet hit the rack, his momentum—he loved that word, just like the Human Who Writes Funny Books did—taking him and the rack to the floor, right in front of the door. He was flying off the rack before it hit the ground, landing softly and spinning to check if it was going to work. Short Guy yelled something from inside the room. Seconds passed. The whirlpool fountain made its water noise, and then he tried to open the door. It stuck. The man yelled again and pushed harder. The rack moved, but came up against one of the heavy wooden chairs from the craft table and stopped.

"Halp!" Short Guy bellowed through the crack.

"Shut *up!*" Big Guy yelled back from the front of the store, but didn't seem to be walking this way. "You want someone to hear us?"

Short Guy grumbled and tried to squeeze through the gap, but it was too small.

Okay, phase one was complete. Now Squeekie needed a way to make sure these guys didn't want to stay here. He'd already made it unpleasant. Now he needed to make it scarier than going outside was for them. And he knew just what to do.

Not all the ghosts in the store were friendly ones.

He ran past Big Guy into the back room and toward the stairs. Big Guy yelled "hey!" and started after him. Squeekie stopped until he got around the corner and could see him, then ran again. His heart thundered. Taunting the thing in the basement was scary for him, too, but he was brave, a defender, a protector, and he could handle what was coming. He halted at the top of the stairs, listening to the footsteps behind him, feeling their vibration, and when Big Guy was close enough, he gave a mournful howl that echoed into the darkness beneath. He waited, his whole body tense, knowing those big hands would close around him any second.

C'mon, c'mon, you always come for that cry. He used to taunt the Being from Below until that one time he stayed too long and the ghost's tentacles had caught him. He never wanted to feel that sorrow and despair again. But if he timed this right...

There.

He twisted to the side, feet scrabbling on the concrete floor until they got traction—another good word, he liked words related to his physical skills—and got out of the way just before the tentacles waved up out of the gloom.

Big Guy shrieked and pinwheeled his arms, trying to stop and back up at the same time. He fell on his butt and pushed with his feet, looking like a big bug, as the ghost groped for him. He screamed again, and from the other room, Short Guy shouted, too, his voice afraid. Finally Big Guy got his feet under him—slower and clumsier than a dog, even, a cat would have been much more graceful and fast—and ran back out into the main part of the store. Squeekie followed him all the way to the back.

"What? What? What happened? Are you all right? What's going on? Is it the cops?" Short Guy was wedged into the gap, one foot and one arm through, but stuck at the shoulder and lower leg.

Big Guy bent to grab the rack and heave it out of the way, and Short Guy tumbled out onto his hands and knees.

"We gotta get out of here."

"What about the cops?"

"I'd rather go to jail than spend another minute in here with that *thing.*" He hauled his friend up by the back of his hoodie.

Short Guy squinted at Squeekie. "What thing, the cat?"

Squeekie tilted his head, and Short Guy smiled at him.

"Aw, he's cute, too. Not as cute at the little one, but—"

"Shut up." Big Guy slapped Short Guy on the back of the head and herded him toward the front door. "Not him. Devil cat," he grumbled, and muttered more things under his breath.

Squeekie Saves the Store

Once again Squeekie followed them until they reached the door. He sat in the foyer archway, watching them, tail swishing against the floor. They peered out, looking nervous.

"Maybe we should wait," Short Guy suggested.

Big Guy looked back at Squeekie. He stared back. He always won staring contests, unless he got bored, and even then he won, because it was a decision, not a have to, when he looked away. This time he wasn't looking away. It didn't take long. Big Guy shook his head. "No. We leave now." He pushed the door open, and they went outside.

Blue and red lights flashed, and a short, loud *"whoooop"* sounded. Both guys threw their hands up in the air. Then they stepped forward, out of Squeekie's sight.

His job here was done.

Anika padded up to him, blinking sleepily. "What are you doing out here, Squeekie? So much noise. You interrupted my beauty nap."

"Nothing you have to worry about."

She licked her paw a couple of times. "Good. Now get me some treats." She turned and strolled away.

Squeekie waited long enough to show Anika that she wasn't the boss of him, and then he went to knock over and gnaw open the tub. He deserved a few treats, himself.

The next morning, he was basking in a sunbeam when his people arrived. He flicked the tip of his tail to say hello and absorbed their pats of greeting, but didn't leave his comfy spot.

"I can't believe it!" Mother's friend said. "I'm so glad you weren't here! They could have—" She cleared her throat and looked at Mother's young person.

Mother shrugged. "It was the middle of the night. We didn't even hear the phone when they tried to call to tell us. I have to look around to see if anything is missing. The door was unlocked all night. But get this. They said one of the guys was hysterical, yelling about a demon cat and a murdering ghost." She reached over to stroke Squeekie. "They're talking about you, aren't they, you clever thing?"

He yawned. It was all in a night's work for Adventure Cat.

Natalie J. Damschroder

AUTHOR BIOGRAPHY

Natalie J. Damschroder is a multi-published author of contemporary and paranormal romance, with an emphasis on romantic adventure. She also writes YA paranormal adventure as NJ Damschroder. A 2012 recipient of the RWA Service Award and two-time finalist in the EPIC eBook Awards romantic suspense category, she is also a multi-finalist in the International Digital Awards, and the third book in her Goddesses Rising trilogy, *Sunroper*, won the 2014 Prism for Light Paranormal Romance.

Natalie grew up in Massachusetts and loves the New England Patriots more than anything. (Except her family. And writing and reading. And popcorn.) When she's not writing, revising, proofreading, or promoting her work, she works as a freelance project manager. She and her husband have two daughters, one of whom is also a novelist. (The other one prefers math. Smart kid. Practical.) You can learn more about her at www.nataliedamschroder.com or www.njdamschroder.com, where you'll also find links to her blogs and social media.

15

Squeekie and the Kitten

Samantha Coons

I woke up and heard the delighted squeals of the Usual Humans. I yawned and stretched out my legs, and jumped out of my hiding spot behind the counter, expecting to be met with the Praise of My Beauty and the Attention Consisting of Pets and Scritches. However, no one stood behind the counter at all. I blinked a few times and sniffed at the chair where the Usual Humans sit, but the excited noises definitely came from the other side of my domain.

I sauntered over to the counter and prepared to jump.

"This gets harder every day," I thought to myself. "I think they must be making it higher."

I jumped and barely made it, scrabbling over the ledge. I peered over at the Cage that is Mine (as All Things are Mine).

The Usual Humans cooed over something in a huddle. I squinted and saw *them*.

Two little fluffballs scrambling around the Cage that is Mine. Kittens.

"No!" I yelled, but the Usual Humans didn't seem to hear me.

I jumped down and padded over, slipping between the Cage that is Mine (as All Things are Mine) and the Usual Humans.

"Return these Kittens at once," I demanded in my most commanding voice.

Human who Smells like a Dog leaned over and gave me a few pets.

"You want to meet the kittens too Squeekie?" she asked.

"No. I don't."

She picked me up, not understanding as they never understand, and held me out to the cage. A little gray fluffball waddled over and poked her nose at me. I hissed, which didn't phase her because fluffballs are too small and dumb to understand Cat (or Human for that matter) clearly.

"Squeekie" Human who Smells like a Dog chided as the gray fluffball cocked her head at me. Dog Human set me back down on the floor and went back to cooing at the kittens.

I prowled away and spent the rest of the day hiding behind the Magical Curtains that only the Usual Humans can enter.

After darkness fell over the store that night, I slunk back out to the Cage that is Mine (as All Things are Mine) and yowled my best yowl. The fluffballs peered down from the top of the Cage that is Mine.

"Hewwo?" the gray one said, once again cocking her head at me. The orange one curled into a tiny ball on the floor, and only the tops of his ears poked out.

"Hello, kittens," I said. "I want you to know that you are in the Cage, which is Mine, in the Store, which is Mine, and that all of the Humans are Mine."

She stared down at me.

"Will you pway wif us?" she said.

I went back behind the Magical Curtain until morning.

Despite explaining over and over again to Mother the next morning why it was a terrible idea to keep kittens in the Store which is Mine, they remained. I did my best to ignore them, they were only kittens after all, and I suppose it was not their fault that they were only kittens. Sometimes Mother talks about when I was a kitten, but if I really was a kitten (which I doubt) I'm sure I was very exceptional.

These kittens were not very exceptional. The gray one ran around the Cage that is Mine playing with anything she could toss, and the orange one hid in the Cave of Wondrous Warmth (which I hardly need add, was Mine).

The gray one called out to me and all of the other Cats that are Not Kittens as we went past the cage. We all ignored the fluffball's

Squeekie and the Kitten

cries, except for Fuzzy Gray who is young enough that he doesn't understand how to handle kittens. The Usual Humans and the Humans that Come and Go still paid the fluffballs a lot of Attention that Should Have Been Mine, but within a week they were giving me an acceptable amount of Praise of My Beauty and Attention Consisting of Pets and Scritches so things were alright until the kittens would go away (as All Cats who are Not Me go away).

The gray fluffball went away after another week, tucked away in what the humans call a cat carrier being carried by a young duo of smiling humans. I think the cat carriers must be mine, but with so many things that are Mine, it can be hard to keep track. The other Proper Cats and I were glad to see the fluffball go since she was so loud and always called out to us to 'pway' as we went past. Unfortunately, the Going Away of the gray fluffball caused all of the Humans to pay extra attention to the orange fluffball. I watched and patiently waited for the attention to come back to me. After about an hour, I got tired of waiting and went over to the Humans.

"Bad humans, you are supposed to pay attention to me."

Human who Makes the Walls Colorful picked me up.

"Maybe he's lonely. Do you think we should put Squeekie in with him for a while?"

I didn't understand what she meant until I noticed the small orange nose poking out from under a blanket in the cage.

Put me in there? With the kitten?

"I think that's a great idea." Mother called out from behind the counter.

"Mother" I cried, horrified that she was going along with this. I should not have been surprised, Mother is the one who lets these kittens into the store. She is the Greatest and Most Powerful Human, and the one that Gives Me the Most Treats. But for some reason, she likes to have other cats around. I'm still trying to figure out why this is when she has me.

Dog Human opened the latch for the Cage which is Mine, as Mother had spoken and Mother must be obeyed, and Wall Human placed me inside. I meant to try and jump out but was momentarily distracted by the existence of food within the Cage which is Mine, and so when I finally turned back around, the Usual Humans had gone and were doing the Usual Human things. The orange fluffball was still peering from under his blanket. I chose to ignore him and entered the Cave of Wondrous Warmth with my head held high. The kitten didn't bother me.

'Squeekie's Not-So-Inner Monologue Part 1:
It has been so long since I have seen the light
Felt the fresh air
Stretched my legs and run free
It has now been
...some...
Amount of time
Since I was put in
But I don't know how to tell time
At least like humans
I am so bored
So unloved
Woe to me.'

Before the Usual Humans left for the night, I was released from the Cage which is Mine. Since humans can be tricky and indecisive, I immediately ran behind the Magical Curtain and hid behind a box, because boxes are magical and safe.

It is warm and soft. My mother is in the box with us. My brothers and sister are climbing onto mother, chasing each other. I watch with my newly opened eyes, tucked in a corner. I don't want to close my eyes, but they droop along with my head, and the world is dark again.

Now there are hands. Hands pull out my younger brother, and we don't see him again.

The hands pick me up. I let out a squeak. Mother looks resigned as she watches me go. I keep squeaking. I want to go back.

I woke up, somehow having made my way into the box during the night. I could hear Mother talking to the kitten beyond the

Magical Curtain. I thought about jumping out and yowling until she gave me attention or treats, but for some reason, I didn't want to leave the box. It was warm.

'Squeekie's Not-So-Inner Monologue Part 2:
They have put me in the Cage which is Mine
With the kitten
Again
My life is such agony...'

"Excuse me, sir?" The voice was small and easily ignored, so I ignored it.

'The days become long
And no one pets me
Or gives me treats...'

"Sir? Why are you talking to yourself?"
The voice was slightly louder now, but it was asking impertinent questions, so I continued to ignore it.

'Nothing but kitten food
And a small bowl of water
Alas
To be have abandoned in such squalor...'

This time an orange head interrupted my refined thoughts. I stopped talking and stared at him. He shrank into himself at that, but managed to pipe up.
"I don't think it's so bad in here..."
I turned around and continued my monologue to the back wall.

I grew to think and take this as you will as I was no doubt severely affected from being trapped in My Cage for so long, that the kitten was not so bad.
He was much quieter than his sister, and he wasn't as pushy. He took to listening to me talk to the Usual Humans as they wander

by with the things they call 'books' in their arms. He would sit outside the Cave of Wondrous Warmth and nap while they went past and I expressed my displeasure to them, not that they ever listened (being Human and all).

One night after the humans had left, he asked me:

"Will I get to stay here with you and the Humans forever?"

I didn't answer. But I let him into the Cave of Wondrous Warmth with me...which made it even a little warmer.

"The Humans are saying your name a lot the last few days kitten."

"I know."

"And not just the Dog Human. All of the Humans."

"I know."

"That is unacceptable."

The kitten yawned curled up next to me.

"I know."

"I want to know why this injustice must stand."

The kitten didn't answer, either because he was asleep or because he didn't think 'I know' was a proper answer to that statement.

The Dog Human (who had grown annoyingly attached to the kitten) came over and opened the cage to scratch under the kitten's chin.

"Hey little guy...I guess you'll be leaving tomorrow. We'll all be sad to see you go, but your family will be really nice! I promise."

He purred. I don't think he knew what the human was saying. But I did.

I got up, and the kitten fell to the side, blinking his eyes as he woke up.

I started eating because food is good and never leaves you.

The kitten watched me for a minute before yawning and going back to sleep.

That night I couldn't sleep. I sat in the cage where I had been trapped and stared out at the store without making a sound. Mother would be Proud.

Squeekie and the Kitten

The kitten woke up after an hour or two and saw me sitting.

"What's wrong?" he asked in his Completely Not At All Adorable Little Kitten Voice.

I shrugged.

He stretched and came to sit by me. For a while, neither of us spoke.

"You're leaving tomorrow," I told him.

He cocked his head.

"Leaving what?"

"The bookstore. You're leaving to live with your forever family. Like all the cats do."

He seemed to shrink a little. "Oh."

He shifted his weight from paw to paw for a moment.

"Do you think they will be nice to me? My forever family?"

For a second, I was about to say "Probably" but then I saw him beside me, small and quiet. His eyes big and eternally worried looking.

"Yes. That's why you're going there."

He seemed calmer but no less sad after that.

"Mr. Squeekie...you'll always be my friend, though right?"

I wanted to scream. I hadn't wanted to like a kitten in the first place. Kittens always go the fastest. I thought this one was different, after being here for so long...but kittens always leave.

"Of course," I told him and started grooming the fur behind his ears.

I watched the next day as his new family came and collected him, how they cooed over him and tickled his feet. The Usual Humans waved goodbye as he was carried in his crate out the door. I saw him watching me the whole time he was leaving. I wanted to close my eyes and try to sleep. But I followed as far as the Humans would let me.

I didn't eat my dinner that night. I lay in the Cave of Wondrous Warmth.

And I missed my friend.

Samantha Coons

AUTHOR BIOGRAPHY

Samantha Coons writes words more or less competently. She edited this book and apologizes for any mistakes.

16

A Friend Like Squeekie

Melissa Ford

Squeekie saw the lady when she walked in, but he didn't approach her until she sat down in the aisle. It had been a slow day and he was sleepy so he didn't want to chase anybody around the store, but when she sat down that meant there was a lap for Squeekie! He didn't always like to sit in laps, but people didn't always sit on the floor either, and Squeekie decided to take advantage of the situation. Maybe the lady just wanted a better look at what was on the lower shelves, but Squeekie thought she would like a visit from him while she was there. After all, who wouldn't want to hang out with the store mascot? Squeekie knew everybody loved him, so she would love him too, for sure!

The lady didn't notice Squeekie approach at first, but she smiled when she saw him and that made Squeekie happy. He liked it when people were happy, and he liked to make them feel that way. It made him feel important to help people. She hadn't been smiling before. She actually looked really sad when she first walked in, like she had been having a bad day. Squeekie thought maybe the lady had come to the bookstore to find an escape from her bad day. Books were a good escape, Squeekie knew.

The humans talked all the time about how they could "get lost in a book" and recommended books to each other so they could share being lost in that good way. Sometimes being lost was bad, like if a cat would get outside of the store, because it isn't always safe for a cat to be outside. Squeekie knew the humans didn't want him to get outside and get lost somewhere; they wanted him to stay inside and be safe. But lost outside for a cat is different from lost in a book for a human. Squeekie was a smart cat and he knew there was a difference, even though it was the same word. Bookstore cats learn a lot about words, if they are clever and pay attention, and Squeekie was a very clever cat and always listened to the conversations happening around him.

Squeekie sat with the lady for a little while while she pulled a few books from the shelf and paged through them. She was trying to decide if these books were good places for her to get lost, Squeekie knew. He watched people shop for books a lot. He hoped she would find some that would make her feel happy. There were a lot of books in the store for her to choose from, so he was sure she would find something she would like very much. The lady pet Squeekie gently and called him a good boy, and he liked that. He knew he was a good boy, but it was always nice to hear someone say so. Squeekie nuzzled the lady so she would know she was a good lady. She probably already knew that, but if she had been having a bad day, it would be even more important to remind her.

After a few minutes Squeekie climbed out of her lap and investigated her purse. He loved bags almost as much as he loved attention. Every bag was a new mystery, and it seemed like everybody carried one, so there was always something interesting for him to explore! It was a small bag so he couldn't get inside it, but that didn't keep him from trying. Trying to get in the purse made the lady smile again, even though she pulled the bag a little way away from him to stop his exploration. She called Squeekie silly and told him he couldn't fit in her purse. Squeekie tried to tell her that he wasn't silly, he was just having fun, but humans were always bad at knowing what Squeekie was trying to tell them. She asked if Squeekie was trying to come home with her by stowing away in her bag. Now the lady was the one being silly! Squeekie told her that his home was the store. He was always happy for people to come visit him there, but he wasn't going to go home with anybody because he already had a wonderful home that he loved. But there were other cats there who needed homes! Did she want to meet them?

But of course the lady didn't understand what Squeekie said and she just smiled and pet him again. She put away the books she didn't want and took the one she chose up to the counter. Squeekie followed her partway there but stopped near Annika, who had been watching them from the end of another aisle. The lady paid for her book and waved goodbye to Squeekie when she left, giving him

A Friend Like Squeekie

another smile. It was very satisfying to know he had made her day better just by being there!

"Why do you always get so close to the humans?" Annika asked him.

"Why wouldn't I?" he answered. "They love me! And they'd love you too if you got close to them. It makes them happy to spend time with me, and that makes me happy too. And this lady was sad, but now she's not! I helped her, and now I have a new friend. Don't you think that's nice?"

Annika made a little noise, like she understood what he was saying but didn't really agree. Squeekie understood – Annika hadn't been at the store as long as he had, and she had different feelings than he did. He was used to being around lots of people all the time and he loved it. Annika's life before coming to live at the store had been different and quieter, so she wasn't used to being around a lot of people, and she didn't always like the attention. Squeekie didn't know what it was like to not love attention, but he respected Annika's feelings. Even though they had different experiences and felt different ways, they could still be friends. Bookstores were full of different opinions and ways of thinking, and that was a good thing! It would be sad if nobody was ever different, and if nobody ever tried to learn from those differences. That was something else Squeekie had learned by being a bookstore cat.

Over the next several weeks, the lady came back a few more times. She always made sure to spend some time with Squeekie on each visit, and he was glad to see her, even if she could be a little silly sometimes and didn't really understand him when he talked. She was always kind, and that was important. Squeekie knew that you don't have to speak the same language to be nice to someone. He thought she seemed happier on these visits than when she came the first time, and that made Squeekie happy. He knew he was doing a good job when people were happy and came back.

Squeekie noticed that Annika paid attention when the lady came again. She watched the lady and how she was so nice to Squeekie. And Squeekie saw how Annika got just a little bit closer each time she watched. She didn't approach too closely, and she always ducked around the corner when the lady got up to walk around. The lady noticed Annika but didn't chase after her. The lady could tell that Annika wouldn't like to be treated the same way Squeekie did, and the lady was respecting that and letting Annika have space. For somebody who couldn't understand cat words, the lady seemed pretty good at understanding cat actions.

Squeekie started to spend a little less time with the lady on her visits, just in case Annika didn't want to get too close while he was around. He knew that it could be hard to try something new and he wanted Annika to not be embarrassed if she wanted to change a little bit. It was okay for her to not want to be close to people, but it was okay for her to want to try it, too. It would be okay if she changed her mind, or if she didn't, but she had to be given the chance to change. Squeekie had learned that from being at the bookstore too.

One day Squeekie didn't approach the lady at all. He was very comfy laying in the sunshine, so even though he saw her come in, he wasn't in a rush to visit with her. He knew the lady would stay for a while, and he would find her later before she left, or she could find him if she wanted. It was never too hard to find Squeekie if you knew where to look.

The lady didn't sit down in the aisle that day, but while she was looking at books on a high shelf, she felt something very soft and fluffy gently brush her leg. She looked down and smiled at Annika, and started to crouch down a little. The lady moved her hand down very slowly, because she didn't want to startle Annika. Annika tapped her head against the lady's extended fingers and walked away. Not too far away, though. The lady stood back up the whole way, smiled again, and told Annika she was a good girl.

Annika liked that. She knew that she was a good girl, but it was always nice to hear someone say so.

It was okay if she wanted to be around people. It was okay if she didn't. It was okay if she only wanted to be around people just a little bit and only sometimes. It was okay if how she felt was different every single day. Annika had learned that from being a bookstore cat. Bookstore cats learn a lot about life, if they are clever and pay attention, and especially if they have a friend like Squeekie, who will let them be themselves, even if that means changing a little sometimes.

A Friend Like Squeekie

AUTHOR BIOGRAPHY

Melissa Ford is a data analyst by day and a voracious reader by night. When she's not doing either of those things, she loves to perform long-form improv. Cupboard Maker Books is one of her favorite places on Earth, so she is especially thrilled to be part of this collection. This is Melissa's first published short story.

Squeekie the Bookstore Cat

17

Squeekie and the Little Horses

Kristian Beverly

Cats were created with magic. Or so they were told. It was handed down through the litters born, a constant hum that told cats that they were special and that while they were capable of ruling the world, it was more fun to let others do it for them.

Magic flowed from their whiskers to their toes and through their tails. It was a soft magic instead of the loud dramatic variety. It allowed them to disappear and reappear without a sound. They could jump from high heights and land on their toes with only a mild soreness lingering. It allowed them to stay as they were, never bending to become different.

The only catch to the magic was following the rules.

The store was different, Squeekie thought. Often Squeekie felt like the ruler of his bookstore. He remembered the tale of the first cats, adorned in golden jewelry and bowed to. It gave them the precision to jump and grab. To watch without having to move

He often felt like the ruler of his own castle with a revolving door of not subjects, but equals. Equals that always eventually found their own castle. Magic, the loud and dramatic type, called to Squeekie but he refused to answer it. He didn't like loud and dramatic unless it was his own voice. He talked to the ghosts when alone at night but always made sure he padded down the aisles, meowing to make sure the humans had left. He wasn't embarrassed of magic, he just didn't want to make it known in the way it could be. Cats were told the stories of their magic and the stories of fallen magic. Humans meant well with their hearts but power had the ability to corrupt and one of the starkest reminders of the whole ordeal was the platypus. What the creature originally looked like had been lost in translation, but the happily beaver duck creature was a reminder of magic gone wrong and forgotten. Especially the loud and dramatic kind. It spoke in screams instead of whispers. It broke doors instead of tapping. And it frightened him when he thought of what could happen, particularly at night.

Today was a new day, and one of the special humans had brought in a tote. Squeekie's tail curved over his back as he moved to smell it. It was different than books, even though he knew his pack of special humans spoke in books.

Today, however the tote was filled with horses. Plastic horses.

His special human held the horse figure, using her free hand to talk.

"See, you can show them and win ribbons," K said.

Two other special humans stood around the counter admiring the model and the case of ribbons K placed on the counter like a blanket.

"It's basically like an art show. You judge it as a moment along with the props and tack and placement," she continued.

Squeekie could smell the outdoors and the places the model had traveled to. He smelled the salt of the ocean and chili. He loved chili when he could steal it from humans.

His first special human smiled before saying, "Ready for the sale? Put them back here and we can go."

K lugged her tote around the piles of books before placing them behind the counter.

The special humans worked in their own way, closing out and turning off the lights before scurrying out the door. Squeekie heard a car's engine rubble to life and watched the reflection of car lights bounce off of book cases.

He sat at the counter. The perfumes and smoke smells that humans wore had dissipated into the air as night worn on. The smell of trees, of dust, from the books filled the air. Annika, his love, hadn't talked to him in days and was still fuming in the back room, so Squeekie had the whole front of the store to himself.

The moon's light reflected into the store and the darkness of night created tall, warping shadows.

Squeekie and the Little Horses

They normally didn't bother Squeekie, but the hum and pull of magic was more powerful tonight. It tickled the pads of his paws. He scratched and licked his feet but each lick left his mouth buzzing like the time he'd licked the hand of someone that held peppers all day.

Why—

Annika padded out of the back room, her fluffy tail twitching back and forth. She moved past Squeekie without a glance. Humans called them siblings, one with more fur than the other. But weren't siblings supposed to act similarly? He and Annika did look similar in the way that crocodiles and alligators did. A part of the same mold with one or two features being telltale signs of why they weren't. Annika glared more than she looked while Squeekie purred more than she meowed. Her feet didn't seem to hurt. She didn't look behind or around herself.

Was he crazy?

Annika moved to the back of the counter and Squeekie turned to watch her. She moved to the plastic tub and nudged it with her nose. Annika's flat face pressed into it again, but the top didn't budge.

A growl rumbled in her throat. "Open it," Annika said.

She didn't add please or even look at Squeekie. Only demanded.

"No, they would be mad," Squeekie muttered.

The much smaller cat turned to face Squeekie. Her mouth was a permanent frown, but it didn't always reach her eyes. Today it did. "Don't care. Open it Squeekie."

Squeekie lept down from the counter. K said she didn't clasp it closed because of fumes or air flow. It was important for the little plastic horses to get special airflow. Squeekie didn't understand how fake horses could breathe, but he'd learned humans had a funny way of caring for fake things.

Annika swiped her paw at Squeekie, catching him at his shoulder with her sharp claws. "Come on Squeekie, or else they'll suffocate!"

Squeekie wasn't sure who they was but he didn't want anyone dying on his watch. He pushed his nose against the top, sniffing it for a scent other than plastic and not finding any, opened it. Then he listened.

Tiny nickers and whinnies.

"Annika—" Squeekie started.

Annika stuck her face into the tub. She seemed fine with live little horses.

"You know this is the bad type of magic," Squeekie said.

Annika shook her head. Squeekie often wondered if the tiny head contained a brain or if it had all been wasted on beauty but it didn't matter right now.

Right now there were tiny creatures that weren't supposed to be moving.

"I want to do this type of magic. It actually does something," Annika said. "And yes, I've heard the stories. I don't care."

Squeekie hissed. It was a weird sound coming from him, as if he rarely ever used it. Which he never did but it needed to be made. He wanted the magic out of his paws.

"How are you going to make this better by the morning?" Squeekie asked. "I doubt she'd be happy about it. You saw the ribbons."

Annika ignored him, her eyes bright as she watched the bubble wrap move.

He moved around the container, watching the bubble wrapped horses move like a wave. A small head popped out, and stared at him.

One tiny horse jumped out of the tub. Her face was small and refined. She stood about an eight inches high at her ears and she flicked her tail. "How?"

Squeekie sighed before sniffing her. "Magic."

The horse nodded like she understood. But how can one understand when they'd never been alive prior? How?

Squeekie grabbed a piece of bubble wrap with his mouth and pulled backwards, exposing more models. A herd of tiny horses.

They ran away from him in a herd.

Annika padded next to Squeekie and yawned.

"You can't be tired," Squeekie snapped. "How are we going to fix this?"

Squeekie and the Little Horses

Annika growled. "Doesn't matter. They're fine and the magic will go down. All's good. Just don't eat them."

Squeekie leaned back. "Me? Eat them? Why would I do that?"

Annika swiped her tail back and forth. "You eat the kitten's food. You eat all of the treats. Why wouldn't you eat tiny horses?"

Squeekie walked away and sat down.

"Loosen up Squeekie," Annika purred. "This won't happen again."

The tiny horses came out again and Annika chased after them. Squeekie paused before galloping after.

They ran and ran around the store, paws scraping where hooves had recently pounded. They didn't ask each other for names, because they would have had to stop and stopping meant recognizing that this would eventually end.

The horses climbed into the tub as the sun began to come up. Squeekie would not miss them in the way they were as a whole. He'd miss them individually though. The magic had dulled throughout the night, like it had finally let some of its build up simmer down to a manageable level. And the horses felt it. They walked with their heads and tails low, feet dragging behind, like they'd been given medicine.

It had been a full night, one that he'd miss but never wanted to participate in again.

"Will you miss being whole?" Squeekie asked.

The little Clydesdale stopped his walk and looked at Squeekie. His dark brown eyes seemed puzzled. "Why would you say that?"

"You can't move anymore."

"I think one night of this is enough to last my whole life." The horse said. "I never want to do this again."

Living would be hard if you spent your whole life stilled.

The next morning K walked in and nearly screamed. Why was the container to her models open? And how on earth were they positioned the way they were?

Kristian Beverly

AUTHOR BIOGRAPHY

Kristian Beverly loves to write and has been writing her whole life. Before being able to write, she illustrated her stories but now write short fiction and novels. When not writing, Kristian can be found on the back of a horse, creating art, or reading.

18

Squeekie and the Mermaid

Lynne Reeder

The day I met the mermaid began like any other. Books yawned as they readied themselves for sleeping all day while sunlight peeked over the windowsills. Dust particles danced in the still air as the front door opened, keys jingling in Mother's hand as she called out to us. I stretched. Annika rolled over, puffs of unruly gray hair covering her eyes. I shook my head and gave her a gentle pat as I moseyed out to greet the humans. Another morning at Cupboard Maker Books was under way.

Hours later, the front of the store exploded with people. A long table held an entire row of bustling, breathing, busy "authors," as Mother kept calling them, and their chatter circled above my head much like it did at night, when there were no people and the books awoke and spouted their stories to the still night air. I readied myself for a boring day of interrupted napping, because I could tell this was an "event" as Mother always called them, and lots of the adult humans would be taking up space today.

As I circled around my bed atop the large wooden table in the far corner, she entered. The cinderblocks of the walls immediately tingled, and my fur stood on end. Not in fright, mind you. More like in anticipation. You see, cats sense magic. It's why I drift on the sea of books' voices every night and know that this little girl holding that tall woman's hand is not an ordinary human.

The girl twisted her foot and tugged on her mother's bag. I inched closer, hoping she would pull the bag free and deposit it on the floor because I love to snoop through bags. People have all kinds of amazing things with them. My movement caught her eye and she glanced my way, and a ripple flowed through her blue irises. It cascaded over me and I closed my eyes for a moment, soaking it in.

Just like when someone pets me just right. I opened my eyes and stared at the little girl. Her smile burst across her face, and I turned to head back to the large wooden table, knowing she would follow me.

I jumped into my bed and circled, tucking my tail beneath me. Her face swam into vision, close enough that her eyelashes almost tickled my nose. "Hi, kitty," she said. Her hand landed upon my head, and I pushed into it so she'd know it was okay to pet me. "You're so pretty. I love your bowtie."

I smiled at her, then meowed. This was the true test. An ordinary human would hear my voice as a simple meow. But someone with magic would hear it cascade, like a slow dripping out of their ears. I watched from beneath her hand as her eyebrows furrowed and she turned her head to the side. She shook herself, as if she hoped to dislodge the last trickling drops of my sounds. I smiled wider. I had been right. This little girl was magic.

I placed my paw on her extended forearm and her attention shifted back to me. Once again, her irises rippled, the ocean contained in her reacting to her movements.

"My mom told me your name is Squeekie." She studied me closely.

I nodded.

"Can you understand me, Squeekie?" she asked. Her hand still rested lightly on my head. My paw slipped from her skin.

I nodded.

"Does everyone know that you can understand them?"

I shook my head.

She beamed, and while I'm sure the adult humans noticed nothing, the lights flickered brighter at that moment. Her hair shimmered and her hand released the space between my ears as she ran back toward the front of the store. As her feet traveled the concrete stretch, they blurred ever so slightly. When her foot was extended down, a shape took form in that split second: not legs, but a severed tail. I gasped.

This girl was indeed full of magic. She was one of the last mermaids.

She came back to me before I could fully process this realization, markers and paper spilling from against her chest. "Squeekie, I want to be an artist when I grow up," she gushed, throwing her supplies onto the table. She reached over to me and adjusted my blue bowtie. I sat up a little straighter. "And I want to draw you, if you don't mind because you're beautiful. Do you mind? I mean, can I draw your picture?"

I nodded, and she shimmered again, a faint glow emanating from her pores, much like the way the books glistened at night once everyone left and they knew it was safe to begin their whispers. She glided into the chair and picked up a black marker. Its scent drifted between us as she drew my outline. I meowed again to ask how the magic felt as it sang in her blood.

"What, Squeekie? Are you hungry? I'll go ask my mom for my snack." Hm. She didn't seem to be able to decode my meow. For the first time in a long while, frustration tied my tongue that I didn't speak the same language as the humans. With magic, she should be able to transform my meows into human words. And she most certainly had magic because there was that blurriness of movement again, that faint memory of a tail radiating around her stride, so why wasn't she--

Unless she didn't *know* she had magic. I buried my nose against my chest and threw my paw over my eyes. Of course. She had no idea the power she possessed. She was only a young girl. She wouldn't be able to control it even if she *had* somehow figured it out. The books in the store only spoke once they reached ten years after their publication date. The younger ones watched enviously as the older ones fluttered pages and spewed their stories through the air. The books kept up front, the brand new ones not even a year old, simply laid there without a trace of consciousness. This young girl must have just begun developing signs and hadn't yet learned to recognize them. I knew I needed to make her aware; what greater gift could someone give to a little girl than her own magic?

She returned, trailing salty breezes in her wake. She held her closed hand out to me, and I peered more closely, sniffing. Beneath the beachy air clinging around her shoulders I could make out my favorite of all scents: treats. Mother must have heard her and given her a few to entice me with.

"I'm Maya, by the way," the little girl said, placing the treats on the table in a straight line. I plucked one into my mouth, taking one step forward to reach for the next. I walked along, munching the treats as she talked. "I always wanted a kitty but I think my dog would not be so nice so we can't get one at our house. Is this your house? Do you live in the store? My mom would love if a bookstore was her house. Books are her favorite." Maya placed the last treat just above the edge of her drawing paper. I snatched it up, then sat facing her. My tail switched back and forth. "Me, I love art. Do you like my picture so far?"

I nodded.

"Thanks!" She picked up the black marker again and went back to work. My ears took shape, along with my bow tie, my eyes, my whiskers. I loved being her subject. I switched my tail some more.

My tail! That's how I could tell Maya she had mermaid in her blood. I jumped down and rubbed against her legs. I circled around both instead of weaving in between like I normally do to people, because I wanted to send the message of her legs *together.*

She giggled. "Squeekie! Come back up here, I'm not done with your picture."

I meowed, my thin voice surging like a wave toward her. Her brows furrowed. "Are you trying to tell me something, Squeekie?"

I nodded and meowed again, circling her legs, pulling them tight as a net would. I stared into her eyes, searching for the ocean I knew was there, begging her to make the connection. I wished she would be here at night, when the books awoke, because I knew they would tell her what I couldn't.

"Maya!"

The woman she had entered with walked toward us. She had her bag on her shoulder, keys jangling in her hand. "Hey, girl, it's time to go. Whatcha got there?"

"I drew a picture of Squeekie." Maya turned back to her portrait, scribbling with her blue crayon across the outline of my bowtie. "Do you like it?"

"Um, I don't like it." Her mom picked it up and examined it from various angles. She looked at Maya, grinning. "Because I *love* it. C'mon, let's go show Michelle. She's going to love it too."

Maya jumped up and grabbed her mother's hand. My tail slipped from around her ankles, my chance ebbing away. I followed her back to the front of the store, listened to Mother gush over the portrait, saw the glory on Maya's face as Mother hung the portrait of me front and center behind the counter. Maya's joy glittered around her.

I searched the shelves as Mother talked about writing and placed books on the counter in front of Maya's mom. There! On the bottom shelf, a row of children's books. I meowed until Maya noticed

Squeekie and the Mermaid

me. I rubbed against the book spines. They'd lecture me about getting my fur in their glue but I didn't care. Time was running out.

"What is it, Squeekie?" Her hand landed on the top of my head. I leaned into her for a moment, and she sunk to her knees, crouching so that we were face to face.

I rubbed the books again.

"You want me to look at these?"

I nodded. She scanned the titles, tipping them out to see the covers. "Oh, Squeekie!" she exclaimed, pulling out a copy of *Beauty and the Beast*. "How'd you know this is my favorite?" Another book tipped over into the empty space left from the volume now clutched in her hands. The end of Ariel's tail peeked out from the shadows. I meowed furiously and batted at it.

Maya picked it up. "*The Little Mermaid*?" I nodded and rubbed against her elbow. You, Maya! You! You're a little mermaid!

Her eyes glinted. "I'm gonna ask my mom if I can get these!" And off she ran.

Did she know? Had I done enough? I sat by the bookshelf, trying to decipher that glint. She handed her mom the books then ran back to me.

"Thanks, Squeekie," she whispered, "for letting me draw you." She glanced back at her mom, who was paying for books she'd grabbed as Mother had been hanging the picture. "And thanks for telling me."

I shook my head, decluttering the words she'd just spoken. Did she say--? But I thought--?

"I didn't want anyone to hear us. But I heard you." She smiled. "And don't worry. I've always known what I am." She reached beneath the neck of her purple shirt and pulled out a shell necklace. As she unfurled her palm, the shell glowed. I met her eyes, and the tides in her irises swelled with the secret we now shared.

Her mother came up to her then, holding out her hand, and Maya kissed me on the head, tingles traveling down my spine before she skipped out the door, adventures calling at her heels.

Lynne Reeder

Squeekie the Cat by Maya Reeder

Squeekie and the Mermaid

AUTHOR BIOGRAPHY

Lynne Reeder experiences the world with a writer's heart and an artist's eye and never goes a day without composing a poem. She earned her MA in Creative Writing from Wilkes University. Poet Laureate of her hometown for 2016, her works have appeared in Mothers Always Write online magazine and Her Heart Poetry literary journal, as well as in the Strange Magic anthology published by Sunbury Press. Poems of hers are among those published in Paragon Journal's [Insert Yourself Here] anthology, The Soapbox Volume II, and Genre Urban Arts inaugural publication. Lynne resides in central Pennsylvania with her high school sweetheart husband, their two energetic daughters, and their quirky pitbull. She spends her days valiantly trying to pass along her lifelong passion for reading and writing to her secondary English and creative writing students, where every now and then great life truths make themselves known--which is what literature is really about, in the end. *Found Between the Lines*, Lynne's collection of short stories, essays, and poems, all paired with pieces of her blackout poetry, is currently available online. You can find more about Lynne and her works at www.lynnereeder.com.

Squeekie the Bookstore Cat

19

Squeekie and the Ghosts

Michelle Haring

All night long I talk to the ghosts, and they refuse to answer me. In my first home, my person left me all day with only the other animals. My person tried to sleep in the house at night. I talked to my lovely red haired person all night long. I told her about my day and what I did with the less important animals. Sometimes she listened and replied. Other times, she said, "Shut up, Squeekie" or asked "Do you never shut up Squeekie?"

I knew this meant that she wanted me to be quiet, but I needed to share my day with her. I was so lonely all day long. Then one day she put me in a carrier and brought me to the large building with different sounds, smells, and animals. The floor felt different on my feet with no carpet to cushion me or for me to scratch. There were other cats, but they told me that they are just temporary. This is a place to stay until you find the magical forever home. I do not understand. I have a forever home, I do not belong here.

This place is strange because people are here all day long and different people come and go. It is like the weekend but better than the weekend. It is like a weekend party. So many people talk to me and tell me that I am pretty. It is amazing. The day is not lonely at all. Then the night arrives.

The people tell me goodbye and turn off most of the lights and leave. The other cats state that the solid people depart every single night. The night belongs to the transparent people who are cold and quiet. The transparent people do not talk to me. They drift away when I try to tell them about the day with the solid people. I wonder why I do not see the transparent people when the store is full of solid people. I think it might have something to do with the lights.

When the solid people leave, they extinguish most of the lights.

The semi-darkness changes the way the new place appears but also the way that it smells and sounds. At night, the bookstore belongs to the ghosts and the cats. I know the people that I can see through are ghosts, and my new home is a bookstore.

My former person told me that I was going to live in the bookstore with her friend. She said that I would be the bookstore cat, and everyone would love me. She did not tell me that I would be alone at night or that there would be ghosts. I am attempting to figure out the etiquette of being the bookstore cat in a haunted bookstore. The days follow the pattern of my first day with attention and love offered by most of the people. The nights are the mystery that I need to solve. How do I convince the ghosts that they can trust me and tell me their stories? I want them to listen to my stories, but I enjoy active and engaged listeners.

First I will count the ghosts. There are three, two males and a female. The ghosts do not seem to interact with each other. One of the ghosts, the malevolent one, does not leave the cavernous, damp basement. He also does not always look like a person. Sometimes he elongates his limbs and reaches around the top of the stairs with arms that resemble tentacles. I am curious about him, but I do not really want to be his friend. He frightens me.

The female ghost looks incredibly sad all the time. Sometimes there are tears running down her face, and other times she wraps her arms around her middle as if she is trying to keep herself together. Her dress is tattered, and her hair is unkempt. She avoids the basement and runs her hands over the spines of the books. Occasionally, I will catch a look of longing on her face as she stares at the shelves.

The other male ghost is my favorite of the three. He appears to be neither sad nor angry, rather he looks resigned to his fate. He wears a hat and overalls with a long sleeved shirt. Sometimes the middle section of his body disappears, and then I see him pull himself back together. He patrols the building at night, and he often stares out the front window with me to watch the trains.

The temporary cats have no opinion on the ghosts, but the temps do not really care about the solid people either. The cats tell me their stories, but I find animals a little bit boring. I prefer people to animals. I am also a fan of mysteries, and the ghosts are the ultimate mystery of my new home. I think I will pick one of the apparitions and make him my communication goal. Perhaps if I

Squeekie and the Ghosts

follow the train watching ghost all night long for several nights, he will acknowledge me.

I am so frustrated at night because I cannot connect with him. The barrier between the worlds is too thick to traverse. After days of trying, I find a wonderful way to talk to the ghosts so that I know they can hear me. Now we can communicate. It is the magical herb that a day dweller brings to spoil me. This first time, it is inside a lovely cloth pillow which I take and hide. I hide my treasure because even during the day it helps me to hear the ghosts moan and I know they see me. During the day, it is too hard to talk to my fascinating ghost. The solid people keep petting me.

I love catnip because it takes me to a slightly different reality. When I am flying on catnip, I can understand the ghosts, and they can understand me. I know when I access my hidden stash tonight, I can begin to learn his story. The first night the catnip helps me to talk to the ghost.

First, I ask, "What is your name and what is your story?"

He says, "I am Bob, the bookstore ghost. I knew that working on building the railroad would be so much better than working on the family farm. My family was large, and as one of the middle boys, I was an extra at home. I was a big boned farm boy, so when I heard that they were building the Rockville Bridge in 1900, I applied. I was 16."

I interrupt Bob, and I ask, "What is the Rockville Bridge? I do not see a bridge from my window."

Bob says, "The Rockville Bridge is beautiful. It is the longest stone arch and concrete bridge in the world. It is about three miles from here, and people come from all over the world to see it. There is also a book about it. The author signed copies when the bookstore first opened. That was before there were any pesky cats here."

I look at him intently when he says the phrase pesky cats, he cannot mean me. I am an awesome cat. Plus I sense that he wants to tell me his story.

"How did you travel the three miles from there to here?" I ask.

Bob says, "I kept my job with the Pennsylvania Railroad after the bridge was finished. I moved with many of the other general workers to haul stone and dig as the Pennsylvania Railroad built a freight classification yard in Enola, Pennsylvania. When the Pennsylvania Railroad finished the Enola freight yard in 1905, I worried that I would lose my job. My job skills were moving stone and dirt. However, I was young, strong, and hard working. These were the only qualifications that the railroad bosses cared about in employees. I started moving freight from one car to another car.

Working on the railroad was strenuous with long hours in all weather conditions. Like most of the single employees, I lived in the bunkhouse near the rail yard. After five years, I was promoted from laborer to brakeman. The job of a brakeman was more skilled than a general laborer, but it was also much more dangerous. As a brakeman, I risked my limbs and my life everyday manipulating the link and pin mechanism and stopping trains with the manual brakes. I knew men that died under the trains and between the trains because all it took was one slip while coupling the trains.

The only people with whom I interacted were my coworkers. I volunteered for the hardest shifts including the overnight shift so that I could keep my job. It was really all that I had."

Bob becomes quiet after this confession. Bob's words make me sad because I hate to be alone. I love people even if they sometimes cannot understand me. I do not comprehend how people can be so lonely. They should connect with other humans because they have voices and can talk all the time. I talk and sometimes people respond to me, but since the day people do not speak cat, the conversations can be rather one sided. It feels like this is a good time to leave him alone because he looks so sad. Plus my catnip is wearing off, and he is becoming fuzzier.

The next night, I jump into the conversation because clearly Bob became a ghost somehow, and I really want to know how this occurred. It may be rude to ask people how they died but I am a cat. I can be rude if I want to be rude.

I ask, "How did you die?"

Bob says, "One night in the winter of 1913, I made my fatal mistake. I got caught between two trains while operating the link and pin coupling. That night was so cold that I had been worried about losing a finger to frostbite, but I lost my life to the trains. My accident gave me a lot of time to think because I was caught between the two trains and the link and pin mechanism trapped me in place. I was actually impaled by the pieces. The type of accident was always fatal, but I would not actually die until the cars were separated. My foreman came to ask if there was anyone that the company could bring to ease my passing. I knew that there was no one that they could call to say a final word to me. I had always been so alone."

At this point, I have to interrupt him again. I want to understand him. His life story and his death story are part of him. However, I really want to know why he is here in my bookstore.

"Do all people who die become ghosts?" I ask.

Bob chuckles at this question.

Bob says, "That is a silly question. There would be so many ghosts surrounding you all the time if that were the case. I believed that I would pass on to something else when the cars separated but I did not. I think that the fear of the next station in my life led to the next part of my tale. When the trains separated, I saw my body fall, but my soul only drifted. I was not free, I was still trapped on earth. I could drift around the yards. I was a ghost. My ghostly range was about an acre. As a ghost, I saw other men die in the rail yards and I saw their souls disappear. I stayed in my acre plot. There were one or two other railroad ghosts but communicating with other ghosts was nearly as difficult as communicating with humans. I quickly learned that human railroad workers really did not want the ghosts to remind them of their own mortality. Many crosses and rosaries had been waved in my face and sometimes thrust into my body."

I said, "The railroad yard is across the street."

Bob said, "I got bored in the Enola Yard. In 1920, my afterlife changed. Within my acre prison, a Plymouth car dealership opened. This meant that I could haunt an actual building. The elements never bothered me because I was a ghost. However, after seven years of circling the yards and watching the technology change, I became bored. At the Plymouth dealership, I learned about cars, and the people that bought them. Plymouth was the Chrysler Corporation's entry into the low-cost car market dominated by Ford at that time. In 1930, the road between my rail yard and my car dealership elevated, and the dealership owners had to build a second level. Half of the building became buried by the construction. If you go into the basement, you can see the plate glass windows that got covered in brick so the original lot could be backfilled."

I say, "I do not like the basement. It is so creepy, and I do not want to talk to whatever lives down there."

Bob says, "The ghost that lives down there has allowed his bitterness to change him into something unpleasant. He does not bother me because he cannot scare me but it is probably best if you avoid him for now. He might come around some day. Here is a good ending point for tonight. I will talk to you more tomorrow if you can score some more catnip."

The next day at the bookstore seems to be so long. I sleep in the front window. I play with a few children. I sleep on top of the computer tower and walk across the keyboard. It is so much fun to make the person typing yell. Finally, it is night time again.

I sit in front of Bob and cock my head to the side. Clearly, he wants to tell me more stories.

Bob says, "As time passed, car dealerships became larger and needed more land than the relatively small footprint of my car dealership. In the 1960s, the Plymouth dealership closed to be replaced by Earl Schieb's car painting business. This business was part of a chain that painted cars for a very low cost. I loved to watch the employees because they did not take themselves very seriously. The employees had fun at work and occasionally in the lower level of the building when the business was closed for the evening.

Sometimes I could interact with the employees that were in the basement after closing because of the special substances that these employees used to party. I also moved their tools and paperwork during the day to alleviate my boredom. In 1970, there was excitement in my building again as the idiots burned the cindor block building to its walls. No one was injured in the fire so no new ghosts joined me after the fiasco. I watched fashion and technology change over the course of the twentieth century. Car paint improved, and there was less need for a car painting business. When Earl Schieb closed, a boat sales business replaced it for several years. After the boat business disappeared, the bookstore appeared in its place."

"Do you like the bookstore?" I ask.

Bob says, "I love the bookstore. The bookstore owners brought a toddler with them and began to fill the space with books. I never had time to read as a human but in my 90 years as a ghost, it filled the time. I honed my reading skills on customer files that employees left open at the car dealership. I worked at manipulating the physical world but my main skill was knocking over piles of paperwork at Earl Schieb. The paperwork was not incredibly interesting but it was words. At the bookstore, I wish that I could open the worlds in the all of the beautiful books. I can read all of the titles. At first there were twenty thousand titles. Within five years of the bookstore's opening, there were over one hundred thousand titles that I could read. A family owned the bookstore, so for the first time in my existence, I watched a child grow. When the family moved into the bookstore, the child was two years old. Over the next seven years, I observed the small boy child mature. Then the cats started to appear."

I squeak in excitement because I think that I am about to enter the story. I like listening to stories, but I really like to star in them, too. I forget about the temporary cats. I talk to them, but they do not seem to try as much as I do. I am the first to care about the special properties of the cat nip. They just talk about when they find their new owners.

Bob says, "You were not the first cat to come here. There were cats here for three years before you arrived. No cats tried to be my friend before you. I did not want to scare the bookstore people because I did not want them to take the books away from me. So I have been relatively quiet for the past ten years. I have told you my story for the first time in life and my afterlife. I think we will be good friends now."

Bob's statement makes me very happy. I like new friends. I know the bookstore owner likes me. She tells me that I am the perfect bookstore cat, but now I have a nighttime friend too.

Michelle Haring

AUTHOR BIOGRAPHY

Michelle Haring is the co-owner of Cupboard Maker Books. She loves all cats but especially Squeekie. She reads approximately a book a day but writes much slower than that.

20

Squeekie and his Friends

Katie Twigg

Squeekie sets his paw on top of the spine and pulls the book off the shelf. He jumps to the side as it tumbles to the floor. Squeekie nudges the book down the aisle towards the counter where there is the best lighting. Leaving the book on the floor he jumps on the counter and works his way up the climbing shelves to get to the catwalk. Over the restroom was Squeekie's secret spot. He picks up a pair of small wire-rimmed glasses in his mouth and carries it back to his book.

His crossed eyes make it tough for him to read so it was complete luck that he stumbled upon them underneath the shelves where all of the children play. They were just his size. He liked to think that he resembled Harry Potter. But just a bit more feline than typically perceived.

After flipping his ears outwards and placing his glasses just right, he turns to a random page and reads:

> *Once there was a kitten who had so many toys*
> *Toys for all of the kitten girls and boys*
> *But there were so many he wasn't sure what to do*
> *So instead he hopped around playing with poo*

A rattling inside the cage causes him to look up. The new orange kitten is jumping around the litter box frantically playing with something. At first, Squeekie can't tell which toy he is playing with, but upon closer inspection, he realizes that it isn't a toy he is playing with. Surprised, Squeekie glances back down at the pages.

This book can't be talking about the same kitten. Squeekie tells himself. That's impossible. He looks down at the title. "Freeway's

Stories."

Squeekie gazes back up at the kitten and calls out, "Hey. What do they call you?"

The kitten watches him for a moment before answering, "Freeway."

Squeekie stares back down at the book again. It's just a coincidence, he attempts to convince himself. He pushes several pages back, heading towards the beginning of the book. Squeekie ends up on a page titled "Matilda's Stories." He immediately begins to read.

Small and black in color. Quiet. Kept to herself. Hid from most humans. Didn't enjoy the company of many other cats. Remained for two years. Until finally—.

More rattling draws his eyes back up to the kitten cage. Freeway is playing around again, this time with an actual toy. But he gets closer and closer to the food and water dishes.

"Freeway." Squeekie tries to warn, but it's too late. Freeway drops the ball into a dish resulting in the water splashing out of the bowl and the cage. The water falls down on both Squeekie and the book.

Squeekie jumps back, startled. His glasses drop to the floor and skid away. The water quickly soaks through the pages causing the ink to run and the paper to wrinkle. Squeekie paws at the pages trying to prevent the water from spreading but ends up catching his claws on the edges and instead tears the pages out of the book.

Suddenly, in a puff of white smoke, Matilda appears before him. More smoke fills the room as Zachary, Jack, Bella, Eevee, and Rubee all appear.

Matilda steps forward, her eyes focused on him. Squeekie can't do anything but stare at his old companion. "Squeekie?" She glanced around sniffing at the air. "Is this the store? What am I doing here?"

Suddenly shrill cries fill the room. The two look over at Eevee and Rubee.

Eevee sits crying, "Where am I? What's going on?"

Meanwhile, Rubee wonders about whining, "What happened to my family? Where's my family?"

Bella walks in front of Rubee to stop her pacing. "Kittens! Stop a moment." She turns to Squeekie. "I want to know what's going on. Why are we back here?"

Squeekie and his Friends

"I don't—", Squeekie starts before remembering the book. He rushes over to it and flips through the water stained pages. He can faintly tell that the only ruined pages belong to the stories of these six cats.

"Squeekie?" He looks up to find Zachary watching him expectantly.

He tries to explain, "I think it's this book. I found it today and was reading it. Then Freeway," he nods at the kitten watching them from the cage, "he splashed some water that fell on the book, and I tried to clean it up but accidentally ripped out the pages. It was when the pages got torn out of the book that you guys showed up."

"So we're here because of a dumb kitten," Matilda snaps. She glares towards Freeway who backs up from the doors of the cage.

"He didn't mean to," Zachary defends.

Jack calls out, "Guys! We need to get back to our homes."

"Yes we do," Bella agrees. All but Squeekie nod.

Squeekie stares intently at the book. He wonders to himself, "So by ripping out the pages, cats can come back here."

"Squeekie?" Matilda demands, "What are you thinking?"

"I can get my friends back. All of my friends can come back to me." Squeekie flips through the pages and finds "Pumpkin's Story." Then suddenly he swipes out a paw and rips out the page.

"Squeekie!" Matilda yells.

Then Pumpkin appears out of more white smoke. Squeekie barely registers the kitten's confused cries as he searches for more of his friends. When he discovers another story belonging to a friend he tears out the pages again and then Smokey appears before them all.

Matilda is yelling something at him, but he doesn't pay attention. Squeekie is bursting with excitement once he stumbles upon another story that he's searching for.

Another puff of smoke and there sits Mac. "What? Squeekie? What's going on? How did I end up back here?"

"Mac!" Squeekie exclaims running up to him. "I've missed you so much!" He snuggles up to Mac enjoying the feeling of his plump friends' fur. But Mac doesn't snuggle back. He's too busy staring around at the others. "Matilda? Why am I back here?"

Squeekie faintly hears Matilda give some explanation, but he doesn't care until Mac backs away from him.

"So much has happened since you left!" Squeekie states

excitedly. "Tons of new people have been coming in with so many new books. I love when they let me sleep in their laps. And a good human brought in a cat tree for me. And there have been so many cats here since you left. And there is a new store cat who stays here with me—".

"Squeekie!" Mac interrupts. Squeekie quiets as he catches his breath. "A lot has happened with me too."

And then they each proceed to tell Squeekie their stories.

Eevee and Rubee practically worshiped their humans. They played with them and cuddled with them and spoiled them rotten. Bella shushes them for they don't seem anywhere finished with their praising.

Zachary and Pumpkin completely adore their human families. They've grown to love them with their entire hearts and don't know what they would do without them in their lives.

Jack excitedly announced that he was no longer named Jack. His forever family named him after some character called Mad-Eye Moody. He declared that his new name is so much cooler than just Jack.

Bella doesn't have many words to describe her adoration for her people. They care for her and don't ask too much of her. They only hope for her to love them and she does.

Smokey can't speak fast enough about his family. They are great cuddlers and feeders and petters and amazing humans. He expresses how much he misses them right now.

Matilda shrugs, "They care about me. They pet me when I want the company. They leave me alone when I want to hide. Their other cat and I get along fine. It's my own space. I don't have to worry about strangers bothering me. It's nice."

A huge smile spreads across Mac's face. "They're great. They feed me, and when my tummy hurts, they just sit and pet me. They're gentle with me, and I love them for it. They always want me to be comfortable. Living with them has been so much fun."

Squeekie brims with excitement, "But now you guys are back to stay, right? And we can bring the rest of our friends back here too!"

"Squeekie," Mac scolds. "You can't do this."

"Don't you get it Mac? We can bring them back. We can bring them all back! We just have to destroy the book. Castle, Sylvester, Smudge, Beckett, Jasper, Creamsicle—".

"Squeekie!" Mac yells. Squeekie pauses a moment, still so

Squeekie and his Friends

excited to see all his friends again. Mac continues, "You need to stop. This is wrong. We can't go and drag everyone back here. No one wants to be taken from their homes."

"But this is our home," Squeekie cries. He looks around at his friends. "Isn't it?"

"It's your home Squeekie. The rest of us stay here just until we find where we actually belong. Our forever homes."

"But you and Matilda were here for so long." Squeekie tries to convince them.

"Because we hadn't found the right humans yet!" Matilda yells at him.

"How did you know that they were the right humans? How could you tell? You could've been wrong."

Matilda sighs, "I wasn't wrong."

"How do you know?" Squeekie asks.

"I can't explain it. My humans just..." Matilda drifts off into thought. All sit quietly as she struggles to find her words. Finally, Matilda looks back to him. "They felt like home. And they still feel that way to me. I love them."

"She's right," Mac speaks back up. "We love our humans."

Squeekie turns away, not wanting to admit his heartbreak. "What about me? Don't you love me?"

"Of course we do," Mac comforts. "You're my buddy. You always will be. But our families will miss us if we stay. And they take care of us. Just look at the kittens."

Squeekie turns to Eevee, Rubee, Zachary, and now Pumpkin who are sitting together trembling.

Mac sighs, "They're just babies. They want to go home. We all want to go home."

Squeekie stares at the kittens. Their tear-filled eyes plead to him.

They really don't want to be here. Squeekie walks over to Pumpkin and settles in beside him. He snuggles into the small cat's neck knowing just how much he will miss the warmth again.

Squeekie pulls back to peek at Pumpkin's face. "You really love your new family?"

Pumpkin nods solemnly.

Squeekie turns to Smokey. "You won't forget me?"

Smokey gives him a small grin. "Never did. Never will."

"We love you Squeekie," Mac reassures. "We never stopped."

"I love you guys too." Squeekie smiles to himself before remembering the torn up book. "But how am I going to fix this. I don't know how to get you all home."

Jack steps forward. "I think I may have an idea." They all focus intently. "Let's try putting the pages back into the book. It wasn't until you took the pages out that we appeared here. So if you put them back then maybe we'll be sent back."

Smokey speaks up, "Is there still tape on the counter?"

"Yes," Squeekie replies.

"Maybe we can use that to stick the pages back into the book."

"Good idea." Jack jumps up onto the counter searching around for the tape.

"We should send the kittens back first," Bella states.

They all agree as Jack pushes a tape dispenser up to the edge of the counter.

Mac waddles over to the cat tree placed just inside the entryway. Smokey follows him and together they push it up against the counter. Jack nudges the tape, and it falls on top of the highest level of the cat tree. Jack follows it down, dropping it from level to level to the ground. Then, Mac shoves the tape dispenser over to where the book lays.

Squeekie flips to where Pumpkin's story was and lays the pages back into place. Mac sets a paw on the tape dispenser to keep it in place as Matilda lifts her paw under the tape and pulls it out and across the binding of the pages.

"I'm gonna miss you Squeekie," Pumpkin mumbles.

Squeekie gives him a small smile. "I'll miss you too." He steps forward and smooths the tape into place, reconnecting the page with the binding of the book.

There's a familiar puff of white smoke around Pumpkin. Once it clears, Pumpkin is no longer there. A few smiles pass around the group, but from then on they all work in silence.

Next, they put Rubee's pages back in place. Then Eevee's, Zachary's, Jack's and Bella's. Smokey snuggles up against Squeekie as they put his pages back into the book. And then there are three.

Matilda looks to Squeekie. "I really do love them. And they love me. I finally found my home."

"I understand. I'm glad you're happy there." Squeekie replies.

"And I did miss you when I left."

"Really?" Squeekie asks amazed.

"Really." Matilda smiles.

Squeekie presses the tape into the book, and Matilda is gone. He turns to Mac and asks, "You sure you won't stay?"

"I've missed you but my family needs me. They would be so upset to find me gone."

"Family," Squeekie mumbles to himself. He looks back to Mac. "Do you think that I'll ever find a family?"

Mac laughs, "Do you really not know? You already have found them." Squeekie watches him with a confused expression. "Everyone who comes here is your family. You love everyone, and everyone loves you. This is where you belong."

Squeekie isn't convinced. "Everyone ends up leaving me, though. Both cats and humans."

"But they never forget you. I can guarantee that."

"You really think so?" Squeekie hopes.

"Why do you think the humans always take pictures of you? It's because they never want to forget you. You make everyone around you smile. That's your gift and this store is the perfect place to use it." Squeekie doesn't say anything. "Just think about it."

Squeekie nods as he pulls out a piece of tape and lines it up.

Mac snuggles up to Squeekie, and for a moment they just sit together enjoying the company.

Finally, Mac speaks up, "I love you Squeekie. You'll always be my best buddy."

Squeekie smiles. "I love you too." He presses down the tape, and the puff of white smoke takes his friend away.

Now Squeekie sits alone, missing his friends all over again.

"What in the world are you doing?" a small voice asks out of the silence. Squeekie turns to find Annika coming towards him from wherever she had been. "You've been making so much noise for hours," she complains. "I've been barely able to sleep."

Squeekie smiles to himself. "Just remembering some old friends."

"Well can you remember them a little more quietly?" she snaps as she walks away.

Squeekie just sits and ponders over Mac's words. Thinking it over, all the humans would light up whenever they would see him. They'd pet him and love him. He suddenly realized that he would miss that attention more than anything in the world. He never would want to lose the love that he receives each and every day.

"Squeekie?" He jumps, startled by the sudden voice. He looks up to see Freeway looking down at him from the cage. He had completely forgotten about him.

Freeway asks, "Those cats really liked their forever homes?"

"Yes, they did."

"Do you think," Freeway wonders, "that someday I'll find a home that I love that much?"

Squeekie smiles at the young kitten. "Of course you will. Every cat finds their forever home someday."

Squeekie and his Friends

AUTHOR BIOGRAPHY

Katie is from Lemoyne, Pennsylvania but is currently living in State College as she attends Penn State University. She is a senior, majoring in Digital and Print Journalism with minors in both English and Planetary Science & Astronomy. In the 2018 fall semester, she began an internship with the communications office of the Eberly College of Science within Penn State. This internship has given her the opportunity to write several pieces that have been published on Eberly's website along with Penn State News. This opportunity is the first step towards the career she hopes to someday have as a science writer.

Katie is an avid animal lover who works part-time in a boarding kennel where she gets to play with many different cats and dogs. At home, she loves to spend time with her boyfriend and their pets: two cats (Peaches and Perceus), a rat (Reina), a mouse (Cream), and a chinchilla (ChinChin). In her free time, she likes to read from her ever-growing collection of books that is currently over 1,100.

Katie was previously employed at Cupboard Maker Books for over two years. Those days were filled with passionate book discussions, adoring cats, and tons of fun. She still loves to visit the store, the cats, and everyone there as often as she can.

Squeekie the Bookstore Cat

Squeekie Celebrates 20 Years of Cupboard Maker Books

ABOUT THE AUTHOR

Squeekie was the bookstore cat at The Cupboard Maker Books in Enola, PA. He loved treats, people, the foster cats that stayed at his store, and Annika. Squeekie helped find over 100 Castaway Critters their Furever homes. After living and loving at the bookstore for eight years, Squeekie passed away on March 24, 2021.

www.ingramcontent.com/pod-product-compliance
Lightning Source LLC
Chambersburg PA
CBHW071358290426
44108CB00014B/1604